PADDLING WITH KIDS

AMC Essential Handbook
for Fun and Safe Paddling

D1166345

Also Available from Appalachian Mountain Club Books

AMC River Guide: Massachusetts/Connecticut/Rhode Island, 3rd edition

AMC River Guide: Maine, 3rd edition

AMC River Guide: New Hampshire/Vermont, 3rd edition

AMC Whitewater Handbook, 3rd edition
by Bruce Lessels

Classic Northeastern Whitewater Guide, 3rd edition
by Bruce Lessels

The ConservationWorks Book
by Lisa Capone, illus. by Cady Goldfield

Quiet Water New Hampshire and Vermont: Canoe and Kayak Guide, 2nd edition
by John Hayes and Alex Wilson

Quiet Water New Jersey: Canoe and Kayak Guide
by Kathy Kenley

River Rescue: A Manual for Whitewater Safety, 3rd edition
by Les Bechdel and Slim Ray

River Days: Exploring the Connecticut River from Source to Sea
by Michael Tougias

Sea Kayaking along the New England Coast
by Tamsin Venn

Seashells in My Pocket, 2nd edition
by Judith Hanson
illus. by Donna Sabaka

Water Trails of Western Massachusetts: AMC Paddling Guide to the Best Lakes, Ponds, and Rivers
by Charles W. G. Smith

PADDLING WITH KIDS

AMC Essential Handbook
for Fun and Safe Paddling

~ BRUCE LESSELS AND KAREN BLOM ~

Appalachian Mountain Club
Boston, Massachusetts

Cover Photograph: Nancie Battaglia Photography
Cover Design: Victoria Sax Design
Book Design: Stephanie Doyle
All photographs by the authors unless otherwise noted.

Distributed by The Globe Pequot Press, Inc., Guilford, CT

Library of Congress Cataloging-in-Publication Data is available.

The paper used in this publication meets the minimum requirements of
the American National Standard for Information Sciences—Permanence
of Paper for Printed Library Materials, ANSI Z39.48–1984.•

Printed on recycled paper using soy-based inks.

Printed in the United States of America.

10 9 8 7 6 5 4 3 2 1   01 02 03 04 05

To Abbie and Hannah,
the greatest paddling partners we've known.

Contents

Preface

My own passion for paddling arose early out of a love of boats in general and only later, as a teenager, developed into a full-blown love of canoeing and kayaking. I remember the summer my family spent on Little Cranberry Island off Mount Desert Island in Maine. I was about eight. I would go down to the dock every day and row a dory in between the sailboats moored just offshore. The boat allowed me to explore.

My cousins had a home on a lake in New Hampshire. They kept a small sailboat, a canoe, and a motorboat there. When we'd go to visit, I would always end up in the canoe paddling the quarter mile across the lake to the beach on the opposite shore. I learned how to make the canoe go straight, paddling solo from the bow seat facing the stern. The canoe was fiberglass painted to look like birch bark. It was heavy and the cheap wooden paddles were a bit too long for my pre-adolescent body. But I loved moving the boat on the water. I loved the meditative feeling of paddling alone across the water, and I loved the freedom.

As a teenager, I convinced my mother to let me sign up for a canoe trip on the Saco River in New Hampshire one early spring weekend. I knew nothing about whitewater, and the trip organizers knew little more than I did. I arranged a ride to the river with one of the other participants (all adults except me). We rented canoes at a local outfitter and, after capsizing several times and losing one boat, we retreated sheepishly to the warmth of a Laundromat and dried our sopping clothes while figuring out how to pay for the ruined boat. By all conventional measures the weekend was a disaster. It was cold and wet. We ruined a canoe and we abandoned the trip short of the planned takeout. Yet I loved it. I couldn't stop thinking about paddling. I was hooked.

—*Bruce*

Acknowledgments

While the initiative for this project came from the authors, most of the ideas, experiences and tips came from paddlers, parents, camp directors, teachers, and coaches who were willing to share their vast knowledge about the subject. Thanks to Gordon Grant for his excellent insight into age-appropriate teaching, Alison Sparks for general information about paddling with kids and for her account of a sea-kayak trip with her young daughter. Jamie McEwan provided an insightful piece on agendas most parents don't even realize they have, and has also been an inspiration to us in our own paddling. Mark Moore shares his knowledge, acquired through years of running the outdoor programs at National Cathedral School, of how to teach kids with different learning styles. Becky Molina provided a valuable perspective on teaching kids to paddle, based on her experiences and her background as an educator. Klaus and Tanya Renner shared what they have learned through adventures with their own kids; Misha Golfman of Kroka Expeditions talked to us about his organization's philosophy and practices in introducing kids to paddling. Ken Stone contributed a piece based on his twenty years of experience organizing and leading school-based paddling programs, Max Wellhouse advised on the section on club-based programs, and Frank Bell Jr. wrote about his camp's very successful approach to developing young paddlers. Thanks also to Beth Krusi and Ellen Gibson-Kennedy at AMC Books, Kent Ford for a piece about the Four Corners kids' paddling program, Bob Gedekoh for his insight into the benefits paddling can confer on teenagers, and Gordon Black for his feedback on various sources of information on the subject. Both Ian Ellison and Eric Grant provided some great photos of paddling with kids and advice from the field about what had worked for them. Finally, thanks to Abbie and Hannah for persevering through our attempts to help them find their own joy in paddling.

Every parent has a short window of opportunity to become an expert on paddling with kids. We have two girls, aged five and eight at the time of this writing, and our lives are intertwined with paddling. But like most parents of young kids, our paddling experience with our own kids comprises much of our knowledge about the subject. Bruce has been paddling for more than twenty-five years. I took up the sport in college. For the past thirteen years we have run a paddling school and retail shop, so we're current on the latest developments in whitewater paddling and, to a lesser degree, in canoe touring and sea kayaking. We run after-school programs for a local secondary school, teaching sixth through twelfth graders to kayak and canoe, and we run a community program each summer for local kids ages eight through eighteen. We also run progressive one-day clinics for ten to fifteen year olds a few times each summer.

Still, we felt like complete novices when it came to putting our own kids into boats for the first time. Hence this book. As we started asking other parents, teachers, and camp staff what paddling adventures they'd had with kids it became apparent that there is a wealth of knowledge and experience out there on the subject. Some of this knowledge is in the heads of outdoor educators who work frequently with kids of all ages over many years, yet do not have the time or inclination to write down what they have learned. But the knowledge acquired by parents who only have small children during a short phase of their lives seldom gets passed on. Aside from a few books on canoe camping with kids, a couple on paddling games, and the occasional magazine article, very little has been written on the subject.

Whether you are a parent, a camp counselor, a teacher, or a scout leader, we hope the ideas and experiences relayed in this book help you find joy in introducing kids to paddling.

—Karen

Introduction

Jessie, a ninth grader at a local high school, had to choose a sport for the fall. She didn't like sports. She was studious and very bright. She was unsure of herself physically and socially. She attended a small school, offering only three sports each semester. In the fall, her choices were soccer, lacrosse, and paddling. She knew she disliked soccer and lacrosse, because they were team sports. By default she chose paddling. She knew very little about paddling, but at least she could be in her own boat.

She struggled through the first fall, complaining and always being last to get her kayak onto the water. The following spring she was back, having chosen to tackle a solo canoe, a more difficult boat to maneuver than the kayak. She stuck with it and over the next four years she blossomed, gaining skills she never thought she could master, helping teach other kids who were new to the program, and developing confidence in herself.

As she prepared to go off to college, we received a note from her thanking us for running the paddling program and apologizing for complaining in the beginning. It was written in a confident, upbeat tone that was much more characteristic of the new Jessie than of the Jessie we had first met four years earlier.

In paddling, as opposed to many traditional team sports, the challenge comes from within, and the obstacles to be overcome are the water, the wind, and the weather rather than the other participants. Paddling allows kids to develop at their own pace and encourages exploration.

All sports can teach valuable life lessons, and paddling is no exception. In fact, paddling abounds with lessons to be learned. As *American Whitewater* editor Bob Gedekoh has seen, "When kids paddle whitewater they learn to stay cool when things get tense and they learn how to get themselves out of trouble. They learn that sometimes it is appropriate to challenge their fears and that sometimes it is better to walk away. They learn to make their own decisions and to set limits for themselves. And they learn not to whine when they are cold, wet, and hungry."

Misha Golfman of Kroka Expeditions likes to set high standards for kids on canoe trips. He feels that on the water the kids can see the result of their work, and that the instant feedback results in lessons that stick with them long after the trip. As he puts it succinctly, "Life is like a river. You can float down it like a log or catch every eddy and surf every wave."

Besides the benefits paddling offers as a sport, it also provides a unique window into the natural world. Grass-choked estuaries, shallow marshes, and steep, narrow creeks all are open to a skilled paddler in a canoe or a kayak. Paddling gives kids a firsthand hydrology lesson, seeing the effects of tides, river currents, waves, and wind.

Paddling is a lifelong activity. If you start paddling when you're six, there's nothing that says you can't still be paddling when you're eighty. There are enough different ways to paddle and enough interesting places to go that the adventure can last a lifetime.

How to Use This Book

In the following pages we have tried to introduce a wide array of tips, techniques, and suggestions from diverse sources about encouraging kids to paddle. Some of these ideas are presented in the main text and others in the form of anecdotes or sidebars. There's more than one way to get kids paddling and we hope that you'll find some useful tidbits. You can choose what works best for you. Paddling is an individual sport and this book is not intended to be a "one size fits all."

Some basic paddling techniques are described and illustrated that will help get kids started in the sport, but this book is not intended to cover paddling techniques in a comprehensive manner. There are many how-to books available that cover rafting, canoeing, and kayaking techniques on flatwater and whitewater but are not specific to children. A list of recommended reading can be found in Appendix E. A glossary in Appendix A defines paddling terminology used in this book.

 Safety is always top priority especially with children. As a reminder these safety tips appear throughout the book, in addition to an important chapter on safety.

#1: The one absolute of paddling is that kids always wear a properly fitting PFD in good condition.

#2: Properly fitting helmets are essential gear when paddling on rivers and in ocean surf.

#3: Sip and nibble frequently to avoid dehydration and loss of energy. Plenty of water and high energy snacks are necessities, especially for kids.

#4: Plan paddling trips and adventures that are appropriate for the age, experience, and ability of the individual child or group.

#5: Always have a fully stocked first-aid kit that is compact and waterproof, and make sure you know how to use it.

#6: Check equipment and gear each time you paddle and always carry a spare paddle.

#7: Be on the lookout for hypothermia—stay warm and dry. Wear appropriate clothing (avoid cotton) and prepare for changes in the weather or a boat capsizing, and bring extra clothes and rain gear.

#8: Pack anything you don't want to get wet in a heavy-duty plastic bag inside a durable dry bag.

#9: Protect children from the sun—routinely apply plenty of waterproof sunscreen (with SPF 30 or more) and a broad-brimmed hat that won't blow off in the wind.

#10: Insect repellent is often necessary when paddling. Repellent should contain less than 10 percent DEET for children under twelve, and children should never apply repellent themselves.

CHAPTER ONE

PADDLING OPTIONS
FOR EVERYONE

Paddling is not a single sport, but a patchwork of related disciplines sharing common threads. Interest in paddle sports has exploded in the past twenty years, leading to the development of several subdisciplines, each of which has its own unique qualities. As paddle sports diversify and more and more specialized niches develop, it is important to remember for kids, all paddle sports share a few basic qualities: exposure to the outdoors, an active lifetime sport, and a great way to meet new friends. Kids who kayak generally pick up canoeing easily and a sea kayaker is usually a quick study when placed in a whitewater boat. There's no one style of paddling that is best to start out in and many paddlers enjoy a number of different areas of the sport equally.

If you're a flatwater canoeist, put the kids in the middle of the boat and take a tour. Let them play in and around the boat close to shore. Show them why you love paddling flatwater canoes. If your thing is whitewater kayaking, bring your boat to the bottom of an easy rapid and let them paddle around in the mild current, or, if your children are too young to handle a boat alone, put them between your legs as you move in and out of the easy eddies.

We focus primarily on canoeing and kayaking in this book, but we also mention rafting in places. Most people rafting with kids do so with a professional outfitter who will guide the process of choosing a trip, the selection of equipment, and the acquisition of technique. For those who are interested in rafting on their own, there are several excellent references listed in Appendix D.

Here are a few of the general categories of paddle sports:

~ CANOEING ~

Canoeing—Short Outings

Flatwater-canoe outings of one to several hours allow you to explore a pond, fish on a slow-moving river, or just fool around near a beach. These outings can expose kids to the joys of the sport in a low-key environment with minimal fear and discomfort. Kids who start out taking short trips may develop an interest in longer outings as they get older, but whether they do or not, they are out paddling, enjoying nature, and learning about the boat, the water, and themselves.

Camping Trips

An extended canoe trip is a great way to take a family vacation. Canoe tripping is also a popular activity at many overnight camps. Canoe tripping can be done with a child of any age, but must be planned carefully, keeping in mind the paddling ability of the child and the ratio of adults to children. The big, stable boats used in canoe tripping can become platforms for kids to play on or, with the proper seating arrangement, kids can sleep or read in the bow while a parent paddles in the stern.

Canoe tripping with kids makes a great family getaway.

Whitewater Canoeing

Whitewater canoeing can be done tandem or solo. Paddling in the bow of a tandem canoe on mild rapids can offer an elementary-age child a great first exposure to whitewater with the security of a strong paddler in the stern. Solo whitewater boats are tricky to control, but many people enjoy the finesse they demand and spend years mastering their subtleties. Tandem whitewater boats are used often on extended river trips since they are second only to rafts in their ability to carry gear through rapids.

PADDLING, CAMPING, AND KIDS—OH MY!

BY CINDY ROSS

Kids love to camp, especially if you start them early. A wonderful sense of freedom and independence comes from living in the outdoors. Here are some pointers to get your family started on this activity of lifelong fun.

Start looking for a campsite around 3 to 4 P.M. and stick to the first decent one you find. No matter how much kids love paddling, exploring and playing in camp rank higher; allow for plenty of camp free time. A good campsite may include a nice place for swimming or fishing, or easy access to potable water. Avoid marshy, buggy areas; sites with thick vegetation; and obvious hazards like steep embankments or slippery rocks.

Use an existing campsite. Teach your kids to bend down and pick up sticks and pinecones at the campsite instead of sweeping off the ground with your feet. This will leave the soil and plant life intact. If campfires are allowed at your campsite, use only down and dead wood for campfires and keep fires small—"toe warmers."

Leave the campsite cleaner than you found it and be very careful not to leave behind garbage and litter in the fire pit or elsewhere. Teach your kids to walk far from camp and water to use the bathroom and dig a deep "cat hole" and cover it accordingly.

Next to your boat, your most important piece of gear is your tent. Stick to a reputable brand and buy from a store with a knowledgeable, outdoorsy staff who can advise you. Look for a tent that is constructed of two layers (with a rain fly) so the tent can breathe. Generous overhangs and a vestibule are good features for a family. Dome tents give you greater headroom for playing cards on rainy days. Remember: When a tent manufacturer claims a particular tent sleeps four, this means a very tight four.

Set up your tent at home before you leave for your trip to make you sure you know how to use it and the parts are all there. Be sure the seams are sealed and waterproof; if not, reseal your tent.

Every person should have a closed-cell foam pad beneath his or her sleeping bag. Check the temperature rating for each bag and don't push it. Also, make sure your portable camp stove is in working order and you know how to start it.

Food, more than anything else, makes for happy campers. Camp foods not only nourish kids, they also provide a great source of entertainment. Children need a lot of food in the wilds—more than at home. Pull out food and drink at every rest spot and encourage them to indulge. Regular snacking keeps their blood sugar level up, their energy levels high, and their moods cheerful. Along with regular meals, let them "graze" all day long. Choose nutritional foods that kids enjoy and let them help in the menu planning to ensure happy eaters.

Be particularly careful of water and always make sure it is potable; dysentery is a dangerous thing in a small body. Encourage frequent drinking to avoid dehydration.

Temperatures can drop drastically after dark; be sure to pack enough warm clothes for the evening and nighttime. Stick to nylon, polypropylene, and fleece; synthetics dry much faster than cotton—no matter what the season. Sleep in long underwear if there is a possibility you'll be cold, and have a hat handy to pull on in the middle of the night. Purchase decent rain gear and know the difference between a water-resistant windbreaker and a genuine waterproof raincoat.

Include some extra activities for the kids. Even if the adult isn't a big angler, bring along easy-to-use, spin-casting rods and reels and bait for the kids. Praise anything they pull in on the line; larger "keepers" aren't important. Kids can be entertained for hours by sneaking up on minnows, snagging them with nets, and storing them in inexpensive, mini bait buckets.

Bring along a deck of cards, a good paperback book for each kid, and a dice game in case you have to wait out a storm or wait for winds to die down. Always have plenty of flashlights and/or head lamps on hand to prevent fighting over them.

Finally, remember to plan your mileage and days according to your children's abilities. They are not interested in the goal, as adults are. Always keep their needs in mind, including the need to have fun.

~ KAYAKING ~

Kayak Touring

Also known as sea kayaking, this paddle sport is popular in areas with large expanses of open water—the ocean, a large lake, or a long, flat river. In contrast to whitewater kayaks, sea kayaks are long and fast in a straight line. They are difficult to turn, but generally stable and easier to paddle than whitewater boats. Some models are designed with significant cargo space and can carry enough gear to support multi-day trips.

Touring kayaks are available in one-seat and two-seat versions. Many two-seaters have a middle cargo hatch that doubles as a seat for a small child. This is a great way to take a young child while keeping them accessible to mom and dad throughout the day.

A recreational kayak used on a short tour of a flatwater river. Photo by Fran Zera.

Kayak Surfing

Kayak surfing in the ocean has evolved into its own specialty with flat-bottomed boats, some of which can be fitted with skegs while others, designed for surfing large, storm-generated waves, are long and very fast. Whitewater playboats with planing hulls also work well for ocean surfing. On an easy day at an appropriate site, a child can sit between mom or dad's legs and enjoy the ride. Ten- to fifteen-year-olds can start to handle their own boats, and by the time they're eighteen, they'll be passing you by.

Kayak surfing is a high-adrenaline form of paddling. Photo courtesy of Adventure Quest.

Whitewater Kayaking

This is probably the flashiest and perhaps the most visible arm of paddle sports, but whitewater kayaking is certainly not for everyone. Despite the impression some non-whitewater paddlers may have, whitewater kayakers are not all adrenaline junkies. There is a tremendous sense of accomplishment that comes from running a rapid in control using good technique. For kids, whitewater can offer a high-energy style of paddling that satisfies their desire for excitement and encourages them to break out of a mold.

There are very real risks in paddling whitewater, especially as the rapids approach Class IV and V in difficulty. All kids and adults starting out on whitewater should seek competent instruction and be realistic about their skill levels and their tolerance for risk.

The two main styles of whitewater kayaking are playboating and river running. In playboating, paddlers often spend hours at a single rapid or a particularly interesting wave practicing various maneuvers. River running means paddling from point A to point B and lets you glimpse scenery and experience environments that are accessible to few other people. The techniques needed for whitewater river running take a few days to learn and a lifetime to perfect. You choose the level of challenge and risk you are willing to accept—from moderate rivers rated Class I or Class II on the international scale of river difficulty, to intermediate rivers rated from Class III to Class IV, to advanced rivers rated Class V and above.

Running a white-water river develops focus, judgment, and self-confidence. Photo courtesy of Zoar Outdoor.

~ WHITEWATER RAFTING ~

One-day and multi-day guided raft trips are offered by commercial out-fitters in many parts of the country. The commitment level can be minimal and the opportunity to get in a boat can trigger a lifelong passion or just get you and your family outdoors for a day. Raft companies advertise minimum ages that should be observed, to keep your kids from biting off more than they can chew.

Whitewater rafting is a social way to enjoy paddling.

Private rafting is becoming more and more popular across the country. With training and experience, you can learn to guide your own boat on whitewater. Private rafters have a relatively high rate of accidents, however, due to the ease with which you can get in over your head in a raft on whitewater and a lack of basic safety knowledge on the part of many private rafters. If you're going to go out on your own be sure to learn from an experienced club, outfitter, or friend.

#1: The one absolute of paddling is that kids always wear a properly fitting PFD in good condition.

CHAPTER TWO

GEARING UP

It used to be that kids had to wear hand-me-down paddling jackets, wrestle with adult-sized paddles, and slosh around in over-sized boats that were hard to maneuver. Recently, however, in response to increasing demand, many outdoor-gear manufacturers have begun designing equipment specifically for kids. This is not to say that adapting larger, used equipment is not a viable option, but now there's a choice. Many parents have successfully retrofitted larger paddles, boats, and other gear to fit their children before investing what can be a considerable amount of money in state-of-the-art kids' paddling gear. Renting gear is also an option and a great way to test different models and sizes. Many paddling shops or outdoor retailers carry rental gear or know where to refer you.

~ BOATS ~

There are many resources available to help you choose your first boat. Paddling magazines publish buyer's guides or beginner's guides that list designs and their specifications indexed by use. Since designs change each year, these guides are updated annually and are a great source of current data. A reputable paddle shop should be able to help you discern your needs and offer suggestions on models. Rent or "demo" different boats before you purchase one.

~ Kayaks ~

Kayaks are boats that you sit in with your legs extended in front of you and propel with a double-bladed paddle. There are a variety of designs sized to fit kids. Kayaks generally weigh less than canoes and kids can usually carry or drag them by themselves.

Kayak designs vary considerably from wide, flat, short recreational kayaks, to sleek, fast touring boats, to super-short and responsive whitewater kayaks. *Recreational kayaks* are stable and maneuverable making them easy to paddle. They come in solo or tandem models. They are great for small ponds and short treks on flatwater or easy whitewater. These kayaks strike a balance between maneuverability and "tracking" or being easy to paddle in a straight line. Their designs incorporate a moderate amount of rocker— the curvature of the hull from the front of the boat to the back. Recreational boats can be used for a variety of purposes such as birding, fishing, or exploring on rivers, lakes, and sheltered bays. They are great boats to start out in because they are so versatile. They are not appropriate for long trips, large areas of open water, or whitewater above Class II.

Touring or *sea kayaks* are used on large open bodies of water. Most have front and rear sealed hatches designed to carry considerable amounts of gear, and they perform well under a variety of weather conditions. Touring kayaks are longer than their recreational or whitewater cousins. They track well, even under the windy and choppy conditions common to open bodies of water, due to their **V**-shaped hulls and almost total lack of rocker. The trade-off for this tracking ability is that these boats are harder to turn in tight places.

Sea kayaks come in solo and tandem designs. Tandem sea kayaks have a cargo hatch that can double as a small cockpit between the two end cockpits, so you can use them like a canoe with a small child sitting in the middle between two adults paddling from the bow and stern. On still water they often are paddled without a sprayskirt on the cockpit. Where there is a chance of encountering ocean spray or waves, a sprayskirt seals the cockpit effectively.

Various types of kayaks (from top to bottom) — two kid-sized whitewater kayaks, a sit-on-top kayak, and a touring/white-water hybrid.

Whitewater kayaks are short and very maneuverable because their designs incorporate considerable rocker, allowing the paddler to turn the boat instantly when coming upon an obstacle in the river. Many newer models have flat planing hulls like surfboards enabling them to carve turns on the river and giving them tremendous stability on flatwater. This new design is great for kids just getting started because these boats feel less tippy than older designs. Since most whitewater kayaks are short and low volume, kids can jump into just about any boat on the market and get it moving, but there are several kayaks designed specifically for kids in the 50- to 120-pound range. Whitewater kayaks require a sprayskirt when used in rapids, but kids should start without one to allow for easy exits. Kids don't mind getting wet; in fact they usually prefer it!

Sit-on-top kayaks are used on lakes, oceans, and rivers and are fairly easy to paddle. Since the paddler is sitting on top of the hull, like a surfboard, there is no way to keep dry and little room for gear storage. There is no cockpit, so you just fall off if you tip over, unlike traditional kayaks which require a paddler to actively exit the boat. Sit-on-tops are made of plastic and tend to be heavy, but durable. They are a good choice in warm water and for kids who are not comfortable paddling with a sprayskirt.

Kayaks are available in a variety of materials ranging from plywood to plastic. Each material offers a different trade-off between strength, durability, weight, and price. In general, plastic or rotomolded boats are the most durable and often the most affordable, but they tend to be heavy. Fiberglass or Kevlar composite boats are reasonably durable and can be very lightweight, but they are expensive. Cedar-strip and plywood kayaks often are built by do-it-yourselfers. They can be reasonably light and inexpensive (if you don't place a high value on your time), but they are delicate, so they are not a good choice for beginners or for young kids.

Keep It Clean

When transporting your canoe or kayak between water bodies, it is important to ensure that you do not unknowingly transfer animals and plants. Both small and large boats are responsible for the movement of non-native species between water bodies and river systems. Although the zebra mussel may be the most well-known invader, many other invader species—invertebrates, fish, and plants—cause significant damage to coastal and freshwater ecosystems. To prevent the spread of these nonnative plants and animals, make it a habit to drain all of the water out of your canoe or kayak, visually inspect your boat for unwelcome hitchhikers, and rinse your boat off with a hose once you return home.

#2: Properly fitting helmets are essential gear when paddling on rivers and in ocean surf.

~ CANOES ~

Canoes are versatile and probably the most popular boats among families. They are big and stable and can be used on many different types of water for a variety of purposes. There are so many designs, choosing your first canoe can be overwhelming. If you are new to paddling, look for a good entry-level boat that will best fit your needs; if you hope to paddle on calm inland waters, then a general-purpose recreational boat between 15 feet and 17 feet long will work. Look for a design that is wide (34 to 36 inches) with a flat bottom for stability and minimal rocker for easy tracking. If you anticipate paddling on whitewater rivers, then a short (15 feet to 16 feet long for tandem, 10 feet to 15 feet for solo) canoe with 3 to 6 inches of rocker is best. By being short and having significant rocker these boats turn easily to dodge the many obstacles encountered on whitewater, but they are difficult to paddle in a straight line. Still confused? Then you need to assess your family's anticipated level of involvement in the sport and your children's ages and talk to a knowledgeable salesperson.

Canoes come in *tandem* and *solo* designs. Tandem boats are usually fifteen feet or longer to accommodate two paddlers. Some tandem boats can also be paddled solo. Solo boats are generally between 10 and 15 feet long and 25 to 30 inches wide so they can be paddled by one person sitting close to the center of the boat. Just as with kayaks, longer canoes are faster and track better than shorter ones. The wider the canoe, the more stable it is (and the slower it is and the more difficult it is to paddle solo). The amount of front-to-back curvature in the hull, or rocker, in a canoe determines how quickly it will turn. Boats with a lot of rocker are best suited to maneuvering around obstacles in rivers.

There are no solo or tandem canoes designed specifically for children. A light, easy-to-maneuver boat is best suited for kids. Two kids can paddle an adult solo canoe as a tandem boat because of their small size. Kids too young to paddle can sit in the middle of a tandem canoe between the bow and stern paddlers. As they grow they can move from the middle to the bow position where they can help power the boat.

An all-purpose tandem canoe preparing to set out on whitewater. Photo courtesy of Zoar Outdoor.

Major considerations in buying a canoe are weight, durability, and cost, which are determined by the material of which the boat is made. The four most common materials used to make canoes are *ABS* or *Royalex, aluminum, wood,* and *composites.*

The most durable material available is a plastic/vinyl sandwich known as *ABS* or *Royalex.* The great thing about ABS is that it can withstand repeated bumps on rocks, falls off cars, and prolonged abuse with little need for repair. Royalex boats usually weigh around 45 pounds for a 12-foot boat and 70 pounds or more for a 16-foot or longer boat.

Aluminum canoes are about the same weight as Royalex boats, but they are noisy and tend to stick to rocks in rapids rather than sliding over them as do Royalex hulls. They need less maintenance even than Royalex and can last for years out in the elements without adverse effects. They are only available in a narrow range of designs.

Wood strip canoes and *wood and canvas canoes* vary in weight depending on the exact woods used and how much, if any, water the hulls have absorbed. The lightest wood strip boats approach the weights of some high-performance composite boats, while an older water-logged wood/canvas hull can weigh 80 pounds or more. Wooden canoes come in all shapes and sizes and tend to be on the expensive end of the cost spectrum. They are great for all types of water except whitewater and many are veritable works of art.

A whitewater solo canoe. Photo courtesy of Zoar Outdoor.

Composite boats are made of layers of fiberglass, Kevlar, or other high-tech fabrics impregnated with plastic resins. Boats made of composites run the gamut from low-end heavy, inexpensive models to very expensive, lightweight, hand-layed-up epoxy/Kevlar/foam core models used by racers and high-end cruisers. (See Appendix B for a comparative chart of canoes and kayaks.)

~ RAFTS AND OTHER INFLATABLES ~

The great thing about rafts is that they are stable, soft, and roomy, and provide a great way to introduce non-paddlers to whitewater. The down side is that they are sluggish on flatwater and some require several people to control them. On easy stretches of water kids can stand up, move around easily, or lie down to take a nap. Most rafts fit between two and twenty-five people depending on their size and how much other gear is in them. Larger rafts are often powered by one or two outboard motors. Inflatable boats are easy to carry and store since they can be folded down to a fraction of their inflated dimensions. Their rubber construction make them fairly durable and relatively easy to patch if they develop rips or holes.

Besides the traditional life raft style made up of an oval "donut" and two, three, or more cross tubes or thwarts, there are several other design variations of rafts suited for different purposes. Catarafts feature two tubes running longitudinally on the outside of the raft (one on each side) with a metal or inflatable framework connecting them. The two, three, or four passengers sit on the tubes in the paddle versions or on a seat built into the metal frame in those designed for rowing. A cataraft, piloted by an able adult and copiloted by a child, allows a child to get right into many of the more exciting whitewater maneuvers with a feeling of security. The third type of inflatable that is popular for kids and families is a "ducky" or inflatable kayak. These boats are a cross between a raft and a kayak, and take advantage of the tremendous stability of a raft while retaining much of the maneuverability of a kayak. They come in single and double versions.

The size of the raft you buy depends mostly on the volume of rivers you expect to run. A 12- or 13-foot raft works well for four to six people on small, technical runs. A 14- to 15-foot boat is more suited to medium volume rivers and will generally hold from six to eight passengers. Boats between 16 and 20 feet are best for big-water rafting and will probably be too large for many small- and medium-sized rivers. Motorized rafts longer than 20 feet are used on some very large rivers primarily in the western United States and in Canada.

One of the many ways for kids to ride in canoes. Photo courtesy of Klaus and Tanya Renner.

SAFE SEATING FOR KIDS IN BOATS

Many families with small kids paddle tandem canoes because there is room for the smaller members of the family to sit in the middle, and room to stow gear for extended trips. A portable seat can provide back support for kids during long excursions. Canoe manufacturers make specially designed chairs that fasten onto the bow or stern seats or can be placed free-standing in the middle. Foldable camping chairs can be used for the same purpose. Be careful that the seat does not ride too high in the boat. It should sit as close to the floor of the canoe as possible to keep the center of gravity low. For shorter distances a very small passenger can fit right in front of a skilled solo paddler and not get in the way. To fit a child into a boat set up for kneeling and outfitted for an adult, try slipping as many thicknesses of foam as needed in between the child's knees and the knee pad (this will raise the child's sitting position) until the child's rear end sits comfortably on the pedestal or thwart, and their weight is fairly evenly distributed between their knees and the seat.

Some parents put their very young children (less than 18 months) in a car seat in the middle of a canoe. The child should be wearing a PFD with a crotch strap. This can be a comfortable way for a small child to sit in a canoe. Just be careful never to strap the child into the seat so that if the boat flips they can float free of the car seat. Once a child is older, bigger, and moving around try using one of the seats mentioned above and teach them about sitting and not moving around in the boat. A couple we met on a multi-day trip out west solved this problem by fastening a canvas sun screen over the bow deck. Their nine-month-old child sat under this canopy, protected from the sun, happy to be facing his mother in the bow.

The middle hatch of a double sea kayak, while designed to carry camping gear and food, also offers a secure seating area for a small child and allows the parent in the stern to keep an eye on them. The child is able to enjoy the view and feel the security of being near his or her parents.

Depending on the size of the hatch, a folding camping chair often can be rigged up to provide a comfortable seat. As in a canoe, be sure that the child can easily exit the boat in the event of a capsize. Keep any ropes or straps neatly stowed where they can't tangle in the child's feet or clothing.

Children too large to fit in the middle hatch often graduate to the bow hatch of a double sea kayak. Here they can help with paddling and begin to participate more fully in the adventure. Unlike in a canoe, in a double sea kayak the stern paddler is too far away from the bow paddler to reach them easily and help them if necessary, so a child in the bow of a double sea kayak needs to be more independent and comfortable with paddling than one in the bow seat of a canoe.

The middle hatch of a double sea kayak puts a young kid just where she wants to be—between mom and dad! Photo by Suzanne Tromard.

~ PERSONAL FLOTATION DEVICES AND HELMETS ~

PFDs

Probably the first and most important piece of equipment to purchase for your child is a personal flotation device (PFD). Most states require anyone younger than twelve to wear a PFD while on the water. *The one absolute of paddling is that kids always wear their PFDs.* In addition to the primary function of keeping a child floating, a PFD's bulk adds warmth and protects the wearer's back from injuries. Several manufacturers offer youth-sized PFDs (see Appendix D for sources).

The U.S. Coast Guard requires one approved PFD per person in boats more than 16 feet long whether on a lake, river, or ocean. PFDs are rated by the Coast Guard according to their buoyancy and their purpose. Type I vests are bulky and contain lots of flotation. They are designed for offshore use and can turn an unconscious victim faceup in the water. Type II vests, most commonly known as "horse collars," are good on calm, inland waters near shore where fast rescues are likely. These vests will also turn an unconscious victim faceup in the water and provide a minimum buoyancy of 15.5 pounds. Type III PFDs are those most commonly worn by paddlers. They are designed for continuous wear in calm water where rescue is close at hand. They won't turn an unconscious victim faceup and they contain at least 15.5 pounds of flotation. A Type IV is a throwable device such as a seat cushion or a life ring and is not appropriate for paddling. Special use PFDs fall into the Type V category. Some whitewater vests are Type III/Vs; that is, they function as a Type III when worn properly. Vests most suitable for youth are usually Type II for non-swimmers and Type III for swimmers.

There are several design features to consider when selecting a youth PFD. Leg or crotch straps are critical in keeping a vest from riding up a small child's chest and over his head. Some designs feature a removable crotch strap that can be detached as the child grows. A collar with a grab loop keeps a child's head floating in the faceup position and allows them to be pulled back into the boat more easily. Adjustable straps and buckles help fit the vest to the child's specific chest measurements. Front zipper vests are easiest to put on and take off.

PFDs for children are sized according to the child's weight and chest circumference. Infant vests fit kids who weigh less than 30 pounds. A child's small vest fits kids 30 to 50 pounds. A child's medium vest fits kids 50 to 70 pounds and with chest sizes between 23 and 26 inches. Youth vests are for 70- to 90-pound kids with chest sizes between 26 and 29 inches. Kids who weigh more than 90 pounds should fit an extra small or small adult PFD. Remember that kids are short waisted and when they sit in the bottom of a canoe, their vests can ride up uncomfortably on their chins and faces. Most designs today account for this difference with crotch and chest straps.

A properly fitting PFD is the most critical piece of equipment for kids.

To check the fit of a vest, put it on the child, adjust the straps snugly, and have the child float in shallow, still water. If her chin and mouth stay above the water and the child can breathe easily when her head is tilted back, then the vest fits properly. Another test is to pick the child up by the shoulder straps to see that the vest does not slip up over her chin or ears.

Another safety feature that children love and can easily learn to use is a whistle. Tie a whistle onto their PFD and teach them to blow it when an emergency occurs or if they need to get your attention.

Helmets

Helmets are essential when paddling on rivers and in ocean surf. A helmet will protect your head from rocks or other obstacles in a river or the ocean. People often assume bike helmets or other sport helmets will suffice for paddling. However, helmets intended for a specific sport are designed to protect your head from the specific impacts expected in that sport. Bike or rock-climbing helmets ride high on the head, well above the ears and the back of the neck. Falling off a bike or a rock face tends to result in blows to the forehead and the top of the head, whereas paddling in moving water generally puts the ears, temples, forehead, and back of the neck at risk. Hockey and lightweight, non-water-absorbent ski helmets can sometimes substitute since they protect the same areas of the head as whitewater helmets. The most important thing is proper fit. A helmet that rides up to expose the forehead or on which the chin strap can easily come loose will provide little protection when it's needed most.

Helmets are made of plastics or composite laminates and are lined with foam or an adjustable plastic suspension system. The lining provides the fit. Most foam liners are glued in and not adjustable, but they can be made to fit most heads well with the addition of thin foam shims. Most suspension helmets adjust like a baseball cap in the back and allow room for growth. Make sure the strap is snug under the chin! Paddling helmets should be replaced after a significant impact due to the possibility that they were damaged in a way that is not apparent, but could weaken them against future impacts.

~ PADDLES ~

Kayak paddles have two blades, one on each end, to allow symmetrical strokes on both sides of the boat. Paddling on one side, then the other creates balanced power that propels the boat more or less forward. Canoe paddles have only one blade and usually are kept on one side of the boat. In a tandem canoe, two paddlers stroke on opposite sides of the boat to produce a symmetrical application of force that propels the boat straight ahead. In a solo canoe, the paddler must steer or "correct" at the end of each stroke or switch hands frequently to take an equal number of strokes on each side of the boat.

Paddles are made of wood, composite plastic laminates, or solid plastic. Wood is smooth, warm, and flexible and the blades often are reinforced for strength, which can add weight. Laminates can be lighter and more rigid than wood, providing high-end performance. Solid plastic paddles are the least expensive, usually the heaviest, and moderately to very durable. Weight is important because kids tire easily with heavy paddles, and the blades are pulled through the water and swung through the air often thousands of times in a day.

Several companies produce kids' canoe and kayak paddles. Because generally kids are not as strong as adults, most paddles made for kids have less blade area than those for adults. When adapting an adult paddle for use by a child, it is often possible to cut down the blade to create the same effect. This does not work well with foam core blades and some other construction methods that produce a less durable core and a reinforced edge.

Kids' paddles are sized just like adult paddles. To size a kayak paddle, grasp the paddle and put it on top of your head. With your hands a few inches in from the blades, your elbows should form right angles (ninety degrees). Kayak paddles are measured in centimeters and range between 150 and 250 centimeters depending on the use. A number of blade shapes and offsets are available in kayak paddles. Whitewater kayak blades are offset between zero and sixty degrees from each other. Whitewater paddles tend to be shorter than those used in touring. Touring paddles are longer and often have narrower blades. They are offset between zero and seventy-five degrees.

To size a canoe paddle, sit in the boat on shore, holding the paddle upside down and out in front of you. Your top hand should be at the throat of the paddle, just below eye level. In a tandem canoe the bow paddler uses a slightly shorter paddle; a stern paddler and a solo canoeist may use a longer paddle. Another way to measure canoe-paddle length is to choose a paddle with a shaft that is a couple of inches longer than the child's torso. Canoe paddles are measured in inches and vary from 48 to 62 inches. They have a grip on one end for the upper hand to grasp and a single blade on the other end. Whitewater canoe paddles tend to have larger blades than flatwater canoe paddles. Blades can be square-ended, elliptical, spooned in cross section, asymmetrical, or quill-tipped.

Which canoe or kayak paddle is right for your kids? Beginners in either boat usually find it easiest to start with a symmetrical blade shape. For kayak paddles an offset of forty-five degrees is fairly standard and takes only a few strokes for most beginners to master. Ultimately, it's the skill of the paddler, not the quality of the paddle that counts. With a positive attitude, whatever paddle your kids start with can be made to do the job.

When kids are old enough they can ride up in the bow, while mom or dad paddles from the stern. Photo by Suzanne Tromard.

WHAT TO TAKE

Here is a list of many of the important items you should have with you on a paddling trip. You may need more or less depending on the length of your trip, the age of your kids, and the season.

- ~ *PFD*
- ~ *helmet (if necessary)*
- ~ *first-aid kit*
- ~ *lots of water*
- ~ *snacks*
- ~ *waterproof bag*
- ~ *warm clothes—fleece pants and tops and a windbreaker*
- ~ *hat and gloves*
- ~ *rain gear*
- ~ *river shoes*
- ~ *towel*
- ~ *sunscreen*
- ~ *sunglasses*
- ~ *insect repellent—with less than 10 percent DEET*
- ~ *whistle*
- ~ *map and compass*
- ~ *camera and film*
- ~ *explorer's kit—magnifying glass, binoculars, nature guides, flashlight, etc.*
- ~ *kid's fishing pole*
- ~ *sprayskirt (if necessary)*

~ CLOTHING AND OTHER GEAR ~

The main concern in dressing kids for paddling is to ensure they can retain body heat. Kids love to get wet no matter what the weather, and their smaller bodies cool off more quickly than adult bodies. Dress for the water temperature, since more body heat is lost from cold water than from cold air. Even in summer, water temperatures on the ocean and on some inland lakes can be frigid. Small kids usually do not generate as much body heat as adults because they don't paddle continuously.

There is no need to buy fancy boating clothing when you're first getting into the sport. When you're outdoors on a windy day, having functional clothing is far more important than having stylish clothing. Again, check with local experts to find out what the typical daytime and nighttime temperatures are in the area you are going to visit and how much precipitation to expect. Since kids' metabolisms are so much higher than adults' their body temperatures change more quickly too. Dressing in layers will help them adjust to changes in temperature or activity. Steer clear of cotton on any but the warmest days because it does not keep you warm when it's wet. Like wool, most synthetic fibers, such as polypropylene, will insulate well, even when wet. Today's general purpose outdoor clothing, which is made of synthetic fleece or pile, provides excellent wicking and insulating value.

Fleece pants and tops with a nylon windbreaker or raincoat over them work well for cooler days. Shorts and T-shirts with lots of sunscreen are sufficient when it's warm. Always be sure to pack some extra fleece and a wind/rain shell in case the weather changes.

For longer trips with small children make sure that clothing has big zippers or Velcro that comes off easily for those frequent bathroom breaks. Hats, warm socks, gloves, and rain gear will add comfort for varying weather conditions. In terms of footwear, kids will need something that can get wet repeatedly. Since it is extremely easy to cut your feet on rocks in lakes and rivers, old sneakers and other closed-toe shoes often are a better choice for kids than sandals. Pack an extra pair of sneakers or light hiking boots for around camp or for hiking excursions. Pack all clothes in a heavy-duty plastic bag inside a durable dry bag with shoulder straps and handles. We have found that a few smaller bags—one or two per individual—work better than a couple of big bags. Each kid can haul their own bag and access it when needed. Pack an easily accessible daypack with items needed throughout the day such as hats, sunglasses, sunscreen, bug dope, rain gear, and fleece tops. Of course, always have plenty of water handy. Attach water bottles with carabiner-type clips to the decking of your canoe or kayak to keep well-hydrated throughout the day.

For whitewater, ocean surfing, or paddling in cold water or extreme weather, neoprene has long been a favorite of paddlers because it provides warmth even when wet without being bulky. Thin, armless neoprene wetsuits made for paddling fit snugly and allow freedom of motion when paddling and swimming. Several wetsuit manufacturers offer reasonably priced youth-sized wetsuits.

On cooler days neoprene provides warmth and wind protection, and retains its insulative ability when wet. Photo by Ian Ellison.

Youth-sized drysuits and paddling jackets are available for kids who paddle often under a variety of conditions. A paddling jacket goes beyond a basic windbreaker, providing snug, adjustable closures at the wrists and neck to prevent water from running down the arms and chest, and a drawstring at the waist. There is even a paddling jacket that can be let out in the arms to accommodate growing kids. For kids who expect to be out in the harshest conditions, a nylon drysuit with latex gaskets at the neck, wrists, and ankles offers the most complete protection from the elements. With a drysuit, no water can get in; the insulating layers you wear underneath it stay nearly dry and much warmer than when they are wet.

Another piece of gear that kayakers and closed canoeists will need is a sprayskirt. Generally, skirts fit snugly around the paddler's waist and the cockpit rim to keep water out of the inside of the boat. The first few times a kid uses a skirt, it may be easier and safer to use a large one that he can wiggle out through the top of. Snug-fitting skirts should be used only when a child has paddled a fair bit and has tipped over enough to get over his fear of being underwater. Then getting out of the skirt if the boat tips over becomes less a source of panic and more a matter of proper technique. It's best to practice this maneuver in a shallow body of water with an experienced person standing nearby.

BE RESOURCEFUL

Before the recent growth in the paddlesport industry, there were few kid-specific boats or accessories. Most kids learned to paddle using adult-sized gear with slight modifications. Younger children are not particularly concerned with which model boat they paddle or whether they use the latest gear; they just want to get on the water. Any boat satisfying that need will do—army-surplus rubber rafts, aluminum canoes, and old fiberglass kayaks all suffice.

These boats usually can be found for next to nothing at tag sales, used equipment sales sponsored by retail shops or paddling clubs, or by asking around to discover what might be hiding in someone's barn. You'd be surprised what treasures can be found this way. Some repair may be required, but it's still a cheap way to get started. Old plastic or wood paddles will work fine and generally can be shortened with some minor carpentry and fiberglassing. The most important piece of equipment to buy carefully is a life vest or PFD. The life expectancy of a quality PFD is generally four to seven years. Eventually the foam will lose its buoyancy or absorb water; therefore, it is probably not a good idea to buy a used PFD that is more than a couple of years old.

For insulating layers, old wool sweaters are nearly as effective as fleece in keeping a paddler warm when wet, and latex dish gloves do a remarkable job of keeping hands warm on a cool day. Synthetic long underwear designed for skiing is just as warm as paddling long underwear, and wool socks under an old pair of sneakers can keep a child's feet almost as warm as a pair of neoprene booties. Just make sure the sneakers can't get caught in the boat, preventing the paddler from a quick exit.

Many of today's top paddlers started out in old, ill-fitting gear and learned to appreciate the sport before the comforts of modern materials came along. The days of old diver's wetsuits, sneakers, and wool sweaters worn to paddle an aluminum canoe during a March river trip are all but memories of the past for some. Misha Golfman fondly remembers making all of his own paddling gear as a kid in his homeland of Russia, giving him a deeper appreciation for his gear than he would have had if he had bought it ready-made.

~ SAFETY AND COMFORT ITEMS ~

Whether you're packing for an extended trip or a day's float on a nearby pond, several pieces of gear will make the trip run more safely and smoothly. Foremost is a fully stocked first-aid kit that is compact and waterproof, and that you know how to use. A typical kit might include the following items:

FIRST-AID KIT

- *latex gloves*
- *a CPR mask*
- *bandages*
- *wound-cleaning swabs*
- *first-aid tape*
- *roller gauze*
- *gauze pads*
- *antibiotic ointment*
- *hydrocortisone cream for rashes and bug bites*
- *slings*
- *triangular bandages*
- *splints*
- *tweezers*
- *an anti-diarrhetic such as Peptobismol*
- *an antacid*
- *a non-aspirin pain reliever*
- *an antihistamine*
- *cold and hot packs*
- *waterless hand cleaner*

Fully equipped first-aid kits are available at most outdoor stores. More important than the proper first-aid kit, however, is training. Having someone along with first-aid training increases the margin of safety considerably, especially on extended trips. The first-aid courses most useful for people traveling in the wilderness, where medical help can be hours if not days away, are Wilderness First Aid, Wilderness First Responder, and Wilderness Emergency Medical Technician.

Water filters or purification systems are necessary anywhere potable water is not available. Products marketed as purification systems remove sediment, bacteria, protozoa, and viruses, using filters treated with iodine. Water filters only remove sediment, bacteria, and protozoa; they don't remove viruses. Treating water with iodine achieves the same effect as using a filtration system.

Most extended day trips require filtering water from questionable sources. We generally start with as much potable water from home as we can fit in our boats. We also freeze several plastic bottles of clean water to use as ice packs in the coolers and to use as drinking water when they melt. When that supply has been exhausted, it's time to start pumping. Pumping water can be a tiring job. To make it easier, carefully hold the pump intake above the bottom of the pool or river from which you are pumping so it doesn't take in sediment. If kids notice the taste of iodine in the treated water, try adding a flavored drink powder to it.

Other things to have at close reach when paddling are insect repellent and sunscreen. Depending on where you paddle and what time of year you go, insect repellent can save the trip. In the north, mosquitoes, ticks, "no-see-ums," and black flies can be so fierce that head nets are required. Other locales are bug free during some seasons. Check with a local sports shop or park headquarters to find out what kind of bugs to expect in a given area. For children, use a repellent with a low concentration of the insecticide N, N Diethyl-M-Toluamide (DEET). Repellents used on children under the age of twelve should not contain more than 10% DEET. DEET should *not* be used on infants under two years of age or on pregnant women. Children should never apply DEET products themselves. DEET should not be applied to cuts, open wounds, or irritated skin and should never be used on the face or hands. For adults, a maximum concentration of 30% is recommended. DEET can degrade synthetic fibers such as nylon, so be careful to wash your hands after applying. Another insecticide, Permethrin, is an effective repellent, particularly for ticks, that can be applied to clothing but should not be used on the skin.

A brimmed hat and bandana can provide additional (and stylish) sun protection.

Some products on the market contain natural repellents or essential oils to disguise the scent of human perspiration that attracts bugs. Citronella, pennyroyal, garlic, eucalyptus, and peppermint oil vary in their potency and need to be applied often to remain effective. Some people seem to attract insects and need the strongest repellent on the market, while others are rarely bothered. With children it is best to err on the side of caution by using a less-concentrated repellent more often. Dress kids who are especially susceptible to bug bites in light-colored, long-sleeved clothing that covers the neck, wrists, and ankles in order to avoid using large amounts of bug repellent on their skin.

With ultraviolet rays becoming more intense due to ozone depletion, the use of sunscreen or sunblock should be routine for anyone who spends time outdoors. Look for products that are waterproof with a high (SPF 30 or greater) sun protection factor (SPF) and full UVA/UVB protection. For kids it is beneficial to find a product that is sweat proof, so the sunscreen doesn't end up in their eyes. The higher the SPF, the longer the product will provide protection before another application is required. Sunscreens should be used to reduce sun exposure, not to prolong it.

An added layer of protection from the sun can be provided easily by a large-brimmed hat. Long-sleeved shirts protect the upper body and arms from exposure. Along with these items remember to have kids wear sunglasses held on by a retaining device; a piece of string will suffice.

Extra food or snacks in the boat can buy needed time when kids are hungry and you still haven't located a camping spot. Gorp is an easy snack to make and carry. Just about anything can be included in Gorp. The basic recipe is peanuts, raisins, and M&Ms. From there let the kids be creative. Ours have included banana chips, apricots, pineapple bits, and pretzels. Let the kids select the ingredients to mix and they'll be the first to eat it! Other quick and easy items to eat that pack and store well include granola or energy bars, apples, oranges, carrot sticks, individual cracker packs, single-serving juice boxes, beef jerky, rice cakes, and dried fruit. Perishable snacks of yogurt and cheese squares are nice treats for the first few days when you have a reliable cooler.

In any conditions, but especially in hot weather, it is important to be sure kids drink enough water (two to four quarts). To make it easy to remind them to drink, assign each kid their own water bottle or backpack-style hydration system. Let kids decorate their own plastic water bottles using waterproof markers or stickers.

~ OTHER STUFF FOR KIDS ~

Besides the basic paddling and camping gear, don't forget to bring other items for the down times or for longer paddles when kids may not stay focused on paddling the whole way. An extended paddling trip is a great opportunity to explore nature with kids. Often kids will create toys or adventures using props from their natural surroundings. If room allows, pack an explorer's kit with a magnifying glass, digging implements, penknife, binoculars, insect or fish net, maps, star chart, flashlight, or small telescope, and nature guides appropriate to the area.

You may want to pack a kid's fishing pole for trolling from the boat or for fishing from a beachside campsite, or bath toys such as plastic boats, pails, and shovels for younger kids. Older kids may want to write their observations in a journal. Keeping the journal dry is accomplished easily by packing it in a resealable plastic bag. Younger kids can be encouraged to draw in their journals even if they can't write yet.

Charting the trip's course on a map and locating landmarks can keep kids involved in the day's plans. Waterproof and rip-proof maps are available for many popular locations. Kids also enjoy recording their observations with a camera. Be sure to bring plenty of film. A compact field guide can help to identify birds, rocks, minerals, stars, and planets.

Marshmallows and hot cocoa are popular items, and books to read aloud or musical instruments can provide after-paddling entertainment. A bag containing cards, paper or coloring books, crayons or markers, Mad Libs, crossword puzzles, travel toys, puzzles, or stuffed animals can provide welcome relief if kids get bored. Older kids will probably enjoy packing their own bag and selecting their favorite games to put in it. Remember to pack things in a waterproof dry bag.

A First Paddling Experience:
Fishing with Abbie on Sherman Reservoir

by Bruce Lessels

One warm spring morning when Abbie was about four, Karen dropped Abbie and me off with a canoe at the north end of Sherman Reservoir in southern Vermont. "We'll meet you at the picnic area in about an hour," I said as she got into the car with our infant daughter. I left Abbie holding the fishing rods while I brought the canoe down the short, steep bank to the water. She followed me, precariously balancing the two fishing poles on her shoulder, looking like an overinflated version of herself in her bulky PFD. She had had brief encounters with canoeing and rafting on flatwater. She didn't love it, or hate it. Paddling was just another way to spend time outdoors with her friends and family.

I held the canoe and helped Abbie in. I took the fishing poles from her as she stepped into the boat and moved carefully to her seat in the bow. I put one foot in just forward of the stern seat and pushed off with the other. I took my paddle in my hands and maneuvered the boat a comfortable distance from shore so we could get set up for fishing. "Do you want to try fishing?" I asked Abbie.

"Yeah," she replied, "but you're not a very good fisherman, so we might not catch anything!" She enjoyed knowing that we were both starting on ground zero when it came to fishing.

I threaded hooks on each of our lines, casted out about thirty feet from Abbie's reel, and handed it to her in front of me. "Hold onto this tightly," I said, "you never know when a fish might bite."

I set mine up so I could hold it in place with a little pressure from my foot and began to paddle slowly, enjoying the warm sun on my face, the surroundings, and the time with my daughter.

We were on Sherman Reservoir along the Deerfield River on the border of Vermont and Massachusetts. About three miles long and no more than a half-mile across at its widest point, Sherman is where much of my two children's early paddling took place. It's small enough that there's little danger of being swept out of sight. The water is usually warm in the summer, it's easy to access from the road, the surroundings are pleasant (with the exception of the defunct nuclear power plant on the south end), and it usually is free of motorboats.

I asked Abbie if she wanted to try paddling. She handed me her fishing pole and picked up the paddle in the bow. She tried to hold it with both hands on the shaft. I corrected her by showing her how my top hand cradled the T-grip. She looked back at me and changed her grip to match mine. The paddle was too long for her. It dragged in the water when she tried to recover with it, and the blade was too large for her. She tried a few more times, then stowed the paddle and focused on the surroundings. I made a mental note to myself to find her a kid-sized paddle.

"Daddy, what's that bird over there?" she asked.

"A blue heron," I replied. "Isn't it big?"

"Yeah."

She looked down into the water and dragged her hand to pick up a twig floating near the boat. She poked the twig into the mud. It stuck and she was forced to let go as the canoe's momentum took us past it. She reached for another and I felt the trim of the boat change as she leaned out over the side.

"Sit in the middle," I warned her, "or we might flip over."

She quickly shifted her weight.

"Do you think we'll ever catch a fish?" she asked.

"I don't know, but it's fun trying," I said.

"There are Hannah and Mommy on the shore!" she cried excitedly. She waved proudly from the canoe as we approached the picnic area.

"Should we go over and see them?" I asked.

"Yeah."

"Did you have fun canoeing and fishing?" Karen asked Abbie when we reached shore.

"Yup, but we didn't catch any fish!" she said happily.

Choosing a destination for a first experience isn't difficult. Your local pond, river, or even a neighbor's backyard swimming pool are all excellent choices. Ideally, find a sheltered spot with little wind and plenty of fun things to do besides paddling. An island close to shore or a beach with shells on it are perfect places for first paddling experiences. Of course, even a swimming pool can be fun to paddle in if you approach it that way.

Sites not appropriate for first paddling experiences are beaches exposed to the ocean or with strong riptides or tidal currents, river sites with significant rapids just downstream, or any site on an especially windy or inclement day. Remember that first impressions count.

Keep in mind that peer groups can have a tremendous influence on a kid's enjoyment of any experience. If a number of similarly novice kids are trying the sport for the first time together, it can enhance the experience; being the new kid among a group that is already proficient at the sport can be intimidating and a real turnoff.

Choose a calm site close to shore for a first paddling experience.

CHAPTER THREE

PLAY IT SAFE

Some paddle sports involve risks that may make parents think twice about getting their kids involved. Whitewater kayaking or rafting, for instance, carries the obvious risks of being swept downstream into difficult rapids, hitting rocks, and entrapping a foot, to name a few. Sea kayakers risk losing their bearings in the huge, featureless ocean, and kayak or canoe trippers spend extended periods of time away from medical help.

As in all outdoor pursuits, much of the reason kids enjoy paddling is because of the challenge inherent in the activity. The job of a parent or adult leader is not to eliminate any risk from the activity, but to anticipate, recognize, and manage any risks the group might encounter.

~ ENVIRONMENTAL RISKS ~

The paddling environment can be beautiful and awe-inspiring one moment and harsh and unforgiving the next. Cold weather, oppressive heat, strong winds, and forceful currents can all lead to hazards that can ruin a trip and, in some cases, become life-threatening. Many of these factors are insidious. Kids out playing in boats under a hot summer sun don't worry about their fluid intakes because the dangers aren't obvious. Similarly, a group exploring a winding river with a moderate current might not appreciate the hazard of a downed tree on the outside of a bend. To minimize the risks presented by these hazards the paddler must be prepared to notice these changes quickly and to react appropriately.

Hypothermia

Cold water and air can combine with wind to cool a paddler's core body temperature below the normal range, resulting in a condition called hypothermia. This is different than when a child complains of cold hands or feet, but such complaints should alert an adult that hypothermia is an impending risk if the child is not warmed up and put in better protective clothing. Children are especially susceptible to hypothermia because they have less body mass with which to generate warmth than do adults. Factors that contribute to hypothermia are wet clothes, lack of a wind-breaking layer, insufficient food intake, and fatigue.

Early signs of hypothermia include shivering, blue lips, slurred speech, and loss of manual dexterity. At this point the condition can be treated in the field by replenishing fluids, putting on dry clothes, moving around to generate heat, and eating a high-energy snack. In cases of moderate hypothermia, it may be necessary to rewarm a victim by putting them in a sleeping bag with another warm person. If hypothermia progresses beyond this stage and the victim's mental state is affected, their muscles become rigid, or their pulse and respiration slow, it can become a life-threatening condition that requires immediate evacuation to a hospital. It is not possible to rewarm a hypothermia victim safely in the field if they have advanced to a severely hypothermic state (a core temperature below 90 degrees).

Preventing hypothermia is simple. The first step is to notice what kids are wearing when they paddle. Everyone knows a child who runs around in a short-sleeved shirt when those around them are wearing winter jackets. Kids often do not pay attention to how cold they feel until their core temperatures are already starting to drop. By being alert to the early signs, adults can ensure that serious hypothermia never develops. At these first signs, stop paddling and insist that the child remove any wet clothes and replace them with dry insulating layers of synthetic fleece or wool. A hat is especially important, since most of a person's heat is lost through his head. If it is at all windy, or spray from river or ocean waves is a concern, add an outside windproof/waterproof layer for additional protection.

#3: Sip and nibble frequently to avoid dehydration and loss of energy. Plenty of water and high energy snacks are necessities, especially for kids.

The second step in preventing hypothermia is to ensure that children eat and drink well. It's difficult to generate much body heat on an empty stomach. Energy bars, gorp-type snack mixes, and crackers are great sources of quick calories. Kids need to snack frequently on paddling trips. Providing each one with an easily accessible source of food enables them to munch whenever they feel hungry.

Even if kids are eating well, however, their bodies will not be able to absorb the calories efficiently if they are dehydrated. Dehydration can occur gradually and it is easily prevented by ensuring that kids drink often and in small amounts. Backpack-style water pouches have tubes that can be clipped to a child's shirt, making drinking water easy and fun. A simple squeeze bottle next to or beneath their seat is another way to store water within easy reach. It is important to monitor each child's daily intake of liquids and to make sure they are getting at least two to four quarts of liquid each day depending on their body weight. A good indication of whether kids are drinking enough is the frequency of their urination. With proper hydration, they should urinate frequently throughout the day.

The final step in preventing hypothermia is to keep kids active. Activity burns calories, producing body heat. If a kid is shivering or showing other early signs of hypothermia, encouraging her to paddle, after dressing and feeding her well, should start her internal furnace going again.

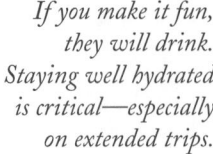

If you make it fun, they will drink. Staying well hydrated is critical—especially on extended trips.

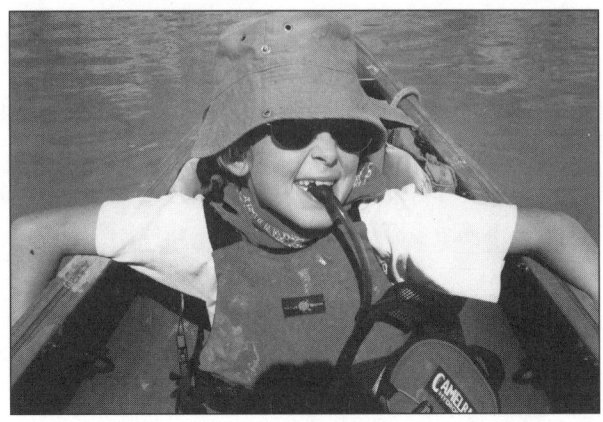

Hyperthermia

Hyperthermia results when the body is exposed to excessive heat and the core temperature rises above its normal range. Heat cramps, heat exhaustion, and the more severe heat stroke all fall under hyperthermia. This can be as serious as hypothermia and prevention is the best approach.

Signs of heat cramps or heat exhaustion, the two earliest stages of hyperthermia, may include muscle cramps, rapid shallow breathing, a weak pulse, cold and clammy skin, and heavy perspiration. As the condition progresses, breathing may become deep then shallow, the pulse becomes full and rapid, the skin becomes dry and hot, and the victim perspires little if at all. All but the mildest cases of hyperthermia require medical attention.

To prevent hyperthermia, dress kids in clothes appropriate for the environment. Under a hot sun, it may make sense for kids to wear long-sleeved T-shirts or long pants to prevent sunburn. If long sleeves and pant legs make them too hot, have the kids splash water on themselves frequently to cool down. Hats are important to protect a child's head from the sun.

Keeping kids well hydrated is critical. See the earlier hypothermia discussion for the suggested daily intake of liquids. In addition to needing liquids, kids out in the sun need to keep their salts and other electrolytes in balance. This is easy to do by adding any one of a number of available sport drink powders to the water they normally drink. Find one they like that replenishes electrolytes and encourage kids to drink frequently throughout the day.

PADDLING-FIT KIDS

Kids too often find themselves in front of their computer or TV screens rather than getting exercise. This trend can lead to a lifetime of inactivity from a lack of physical fitness. Being physically fit not only strengthens muscles, helps in easy breathing, and gets the blood pumping; it increases self-esteem and self-confidence and gives kids an extra boost when dealing with stressful situations.

Paddling, along with eating healthy and getting plenty of zzzzs, is a fun way to start kids on a healthy path for life. Paddling gives arms, shoulders, and torsos a workout, and legs, hips, and feet benefit as kids work to control their boat. As with any physical activity, warming up before paddling is essential for getting the heart rate up and muscles warm and flexible, so that your kids are ready to take on those mighty strokes.

Have kids jog in place, do jumping jacks, or play tag. After a few minutes, switch to stretching. Stretching reduces the chance of injury to muscles and joints. Stretch first one arm and then the other above the head, bending at the elbow to touch the back. Move the torso to one side and then the other. Bend over and grab hold of the ankles. Hold one knee up toward the chest and then the other. Remember to hold all stretches for at least ten seconds, so that muscles can elongate and become more flexible.

Tailor a stretching program to your kids and, of course, keep it fun. Kids probably won't even notice that they are developing healthy habits that will last them a lifetime. For more information on fitness for kids, visit the President's Council on Physical Fitness and Sports at www.fitness.gov.

Tides

The effects of ocean tides range from subtle to spectacular. The change from low to high tide may mean the level of the ocean merely rises several feet on a nearby beach. A few miles away, however, the same effect may be exaggerated by a narrow channel between two headlands, causing a current so strong that it is impossible to oppose and can present a serious threat to paddlers. The irony is that in a few hours the same spot may be calm as a lake on a windless morning, as the tide reaches its peak and prepares to reverse itself.

A full discussion of tidal effects is beyond the scope of this book. If you plan to paddle anywhere on the ocean or on a river or estuary that is connected to the ocean, it is critical to research the effects of the tides before you go. Local newspapers often print charts showing the times of high and low tides for each day of the coming week or month, and local outfitters or marinas can be good sources of information about the specific effects to expect in the area you plan to travel. Trips that depend on precisely timing your movements to the tides are best left for older kids and adults who can understand the importance of moving at the appropriate time.

River Hazards

Rivers change as frequently as the seasons. They often flood in spring, dry up in summer, and freeze in winter. As often as their character changes, so do the hazards they present.

The power of a fast-moving current is difficult to understand until you are caught against an obstruction with the force of the current holding you there. Often despite your best efforts you are unable to free yourself. If you allow the boat to fill with water, it will sometimes collapse around the obstruction, taking the shape of the obstruction as a wrecked car wraps itself around a tree. Appreciating this force helps a paddler see the danger in trees that have fallen into the river, causing a hazard known as a strainer.

Anything that allows water to pass through but prevents solid objects from doing so is a strainer. Midriver rocks also can pin a boat, though most rocks form solid obstructions, forcing both the water and any boat it carries to move around them. Rocks often have a protective "pillow" of water on their upstream sides that can prevent a boat from pinning in the first place. Bridge abutments also can be dangerous, due to their often sharp upstream profiles that can snag a boat and other debris.

Strainers, rocks, bridge abutments, and any other obstructions are best dealt with in the same way—by avoiding them. If you find yourself moving toward a rock or other obstruction that you cannot avoid, lean your boat toward the obstruction. This may be counterintuitive since the obstruction is what you are trying to avoid, but by leaning toward the obstruction you keep the upstream edge of the boat out of the water so the current cannot grab it and flip you over.

Human-made dams and very smooth natural ledges can create another hazard for river runners. Depending on the shape of the dam or ledge, it may form a white, foamy reversal as the water rushes over it, known as a hole or a hydraulic. In a hole the water on the surface rushes back upstream toward the obstruction. Holes are common in rapids of any sort and their white foam is what gives whitewater its name. Most holes are harmless and simply indicate the presence of a rock or ledge upstream.

The holes to be concerned about are those that are smooth and well formed, offering few or no breaks in the strong upstream-rushing current.

A low-head dam with a dangerous hole below.

Another indication of a dangerous hole is recirculation from a significant distance (three or four feet or more) downstream of the object.

In the case of low-head dams, which may drop as little as a couple of feet, the reversal can extend twenty feet or more downstream of the dam face. The danger these holes present is that they tend to trap floating objects such as canoes, kayaks, rafts, or swimmers and recirculate them violently. As with strainers, the best and often only way to avoid a tragedy with a low-head dam or a dangerous natural hole is to recognize it and avoid it.

Some of these hazards are difficult to see from river level, yet there are telltale signs that signal their existence as you approach. Debris piles anywhere on a river should put a group on alert for the presence of strainers. A smooth, subtle horizon line ahead may warn of an approaching ledge or dam. In any case, if you are not sure what is downstream and cannot see far enough ahead to determine whether any hazards exist, it is time to pull over, walk downstream along the shore, and scout.

Scouting from shore allows a group to see any hazards ahead and to choose whether to run the rapid or to portage the section in question. It is also a great way to teach kids about whitewater features and hazards, since a shore-level view gives them a much clearer picture of what lies ahead than a river-level view. Kids should be brought into the decision of whether to run a rapid, but the final decision always rests with the adult leaders.

～ AN OUNCE OF PREVENTION ～

Matching an individual or group to a risk-appropriate paddling experience is the job of the adult leaders, though it can be done in conjunction with the kids. A whitewater trip can be scary for young children, but perfect for older kids with more experience.

The paddling trip itself is not inherently dangerous; most accidents happen because the particular group is not up to the challenges of the trip. It is easy as an adult leader to let your personal ambitions influence your choice of a trip. When kids are involved you owe it to them to take their actual abilities and attention spans into account. By carefully choosing and researching a destination, you can ensure that the stage is set for a wonderful adventure rather than an unpleasant, if not tragic, misadventure.

A Prerequisite to Paddling: Comfort in the Water

No matter what age your kids learn to paddle, they'll need to be comfortable in the water to really love the sport. At age five, Abbie had been struggling with putting her face in the water. That summer we borrowed a friend's kayak, sized especially for children, for her to use on a lake during our vacation. She was nervous getting into it, promptly tipped over, cried, and walked away vowing never to kayak again.

What a difference a year can make in the development of a young child. The next summer after Abbie conquered her fear and began swimming underwater, we again tried her in a kayak. Having learned the hard way about tippy boats, we put her in a wider kayak with significant volume and stability. She loved it and paddled easily around in front of the dock. The added support of her seven-year-old cousin paddling a kayak nearby helped Abbie's confidence.

Sometimes things work the other way around: getting a young child paddling can help overcome his fear of swimming. A friend's four-year-old son didn't want to learn to swim. His parents found it difficult to motivate him to do anything around the water until they started taking him paddling. They brought him first in their canoe and later in a kayak of his own. The paddling piqued his interest in the water in general. Shortly after he started paddling with his parents, he became a motivated swimming student and is now quite comfortable in the water. According to his mom, if they had waited to start him paddling until he was perfectly comfortable in the water, they might never have started. On the other hand, they made sure that his early paddling experiences were very controlled and safe, so there was minimal chance of him ending up in the water unexpectedly.

Even kids who are excellent swimmers need to wear PFDs whenever they are in a boat. Many states have passed laws mandating that children under twelve wear PFDs in any type of watercraft. Children who are strong swimmers may be able to handle themselves under normal conditions—warm air and water temperatures. When the water and air are cold, however, children dressed in long pants and long-sleeved shirts or sweaters may find their swimming ability counts for little if the boat capsizes.

Adult Comfort Around the Water

While it is important that kids who paddle develop a comfort in and around the water, it is equally, if not more important, that the adults who go with them be confident in the water. No one can credibly claim that they will never flip even in the calmest conditions on a smooth lake. In the event of a flip, it is the adults who need to be calm, confident, and in charge of the situation so it can be handled quickly and without anyone panicking. If the kids sense that you know what you are doing, they will be more likely to act calmly and according to the rules you have taught them. If they sense you are panicked, they will pick up on your reaction and panic themselves.

If you are thinking of starting to paddle with kids and are not a competent swimmer, now is a great time to take swimming lessons and develop that confidence. If you have always had a lingering fear of swimming in whitewater, practice swimming an easy rapid so that if you end up in that situation with a child, you are able to handle the situation confidently.

Teaching and Modeling Judgment

The limits of what is safe, sane, or reasonable to paddle have been pushed well beyond where they were thirty years ago due to improvements in equipment and techniques. Some kayak surfers go out in search of difficult currents, tides, and weather conditions. Whitewater boaters have run waterfalls up to one hundred feet high. When do you tell your budding paddler to stop? In some kids the instinct for self-preservation is not nearly as strong as their parents would like it to be. While you want them to develop their own abilities to judge, you also need to remember that as the parent or leader, the ultimate responsibility for decision making rests on your shoulders.

Beware of telling kids to "do as I say, not as I do." If you arrive at a beach for a day of sea kayaking and find the surf is larger than they can handle, but offers a tempting challenge to your greater strength and experience, don't tell them they shouldn't go paddling because of the hazards and then go paddling yourself. This sends a very mixed message. Leaving both of your boats on the car and driving to a more protected bay to paddle tells them you are committed to using good judgment, even if it means forgoing your own paddling ambitions for the moment.

MY LESSON IN JUDGMENT

BY BRUCE LESSELS

At eighteen I went to Canada to raft guide for the summer. I had been paddling for four years on progressively more difficult New England rivers. My skills were improving rapidly, my confidence was high, and mortality was the furthest thing from my mind as I prepared to run the Ottawa River, a high-volume, intermediate-to-expert whitewater run at normal water levels. The river was flowing at several times the normal volume and the waves were bigger than I had ever seen before—the largest topped fifteen feet.

All went well until the last big rapid. I ran to the right of the largest waves in the center, then went to cut back to the left to avoid a large ledge just below the last wave. I started my maneuver too late, and to this day I can clearly see in my mind the lip of the falls as I dropped into the monstrous hole. Needless to say I was lucky enough to be spit out, sputtering and gasping for air. I swam to shore as my friend pushed my boat to shore. I sat there and shook for a half-hour from the cold of the water and the shock of considering what could have happened. It was a tough and very dangerous way to learn judgment.

CHAPTER FOUR

TEACHING KIDS, 101

~ GETTING THEIR ATTENTION ~

There are as many different ideas about how best to teach kids to paddle as there are teachers. Many of the ideas will sound familiar to anyone involved in teaching kids any activity. Most agree that frequent praise is critical. Small group sizes on the water (five or fewer boats in a group with one or two instructors per group) provide a level of safety and an ability to give individual attention that is not possible with larger groups. The great thing about kids is that they are like sponges—put them near water and they will absorb.

No matter what your educational philosophy, as Becky Molina believes, the proof is in the pudding: "Teaching is not merely the practice of presenting material, but rather ensures that learning will occur. If students can leave the class performing a skill on their own, without the instructor, practicing the skill correctly and applying it when necessary to new situations, and perhaps even able to teach the skill to others, then we can be sure that learning has occurred."

Becky has developed some overarching principles that have proven to work well when teaching kids:

~ *Hands-on:* Most kids are hands-on learners; they tend to be better than adults at playing, and they are good at figuring out things if guided and allowed to do so. For example, if you demonstrate a stroke and have kids practice it, they often can give you examples of when the stroke might be useful, then even go further to suggest on their own how a complementary stroke would serve the same purpose in the other direction. Kids are usually quicker at this than adults.

~ *Language:* We can't teach kids without changing the language we use with them. Our kid language needs to be limited (do more, talk less), age-appropriate (six-year-olds may not understand "parallel" and "perpendicular," for example), and consistent (not using multiple terms for the same thing).

~ *Focus attention:* Kids are more prone than adults to distraction, so the instruction needs to be exciting and focused. Multiplying a child's age by two gives a rough idea of their attention span in minutes. So with ten-year-olds, the activity should change approximately every twenty minutes.

~ *Encouragement:* Most kids are not practiced in separating their social and emotional needs from the task at hand. They need "down time" to hang out with peers and recharge. They need to be treated with respect, encouragement, and a high level of enthusiasm.

LESSONS IN LEARNING

BY MARK MOORE

While on the river recently I saw an acquaintance, Jim, kayaking with his three children. There is something very beautiful about a family paddling together. For parents who paddle, sharing their love of boating and watching their kids develop skills and confidence are cherished moments of life. Occasionally, however, it seems parents are barely on the same planet with their kids—let alone the same river.

As I watched Jim, he was doing his best to introduce peel outs to his kids. His explanation was clear and thorough, but his patience was waning. Bobby, eleven, kept watching another group of paddlers zip from eddy to eddy. Tina, twelve, was mesmerized by her hand sliding through the passing current. Jenny, fifteen, was paddling her boat furiously toward the eddy line. To get their attention, Jim raised his voice as he continued his explanation. Unfortunately, he succeeded only in pulling the kids away from their learning, which had been going well but had nothing to do with his lecture.

People gather the information they need to learn through their senses: eyes (visual), bodily motion or sensations (kinesthetic), and ears (auditory). Though learners may respond to any learning cue, often they lean toward one. Critical elements of effective teaching include: understanding that individuals learn in different ways, recognizing each student's personal learning style, and effectively addressing personal style. During Jim's peel-out lesson, his kids gave him plenty of clues; unfortunately, he missed these clues entirely.

Bobby collects information with his eyes by watching other paddlers. While on the river that day, he could see how paddlers moved, how they placed their paddles, and what happened when their boats interacted with various water features. To learn best, Bobby needs to develop an image of what he is going to do and how things work. He thrives on physical demonstrations of skills and techniques.

Drawings, videos, diagrams, and descriptions that create images also are useful for Bobby. I often have this type of learner paddle right behind an instructor or better paddler, offering a needed visual reference.

While Tina was sliding her hand through the water, she could feel the force of the current pull back, making her muscles flex in her arm, shoulder, and back. She discovered that a change in the angle of her hand in relation to the current caused a corresponding change in the pressure on her hand. The more she experimented, the more she discovered. Tina is what many call a feeler. As a kinesthetic learner, she learns by experiencing and evaluating each experience. She may master paddling rather quickly, because of her acute physical awareness. I like to take this type of learner swimming in the current, teaching basic river maneuvers (eddy turns and peel outs) while swimming before trying them in the boat. These kids will require plenty of practice time and minimal analytical discussion.

Jenny's first thought is 'go' when she approaches something new—or anything for that matter. Getting out and doing it is the way Jenny really likes to learn, which is why learners like her often are referred to as doers. Sitting still for dad's lecture is a near impossibility for her. Kids like Jenny prefer stimuli created through their actions. They are kinesthetic, but may not be as sensitive to variations in experience, often repeating the same mistakes. Doers can be irrepressible, and an instructor's biggest challenge may be helping them avoid injury. With a group of doers, I often just get them in boats and let them hand paddle or move on to the next step with minimal explanation. When a doer seems stalled in their progress, I ask if they want a tip to make things easier; they soon ask for tips at the start of each practice session.

Of course, do not forget Jim. He is an engineer. Very analytical and thorough, Jim loves to discuss paddling techniques in great detail and he reads everything about paddling. Jim is an auditory learner; he likes detailed explanations to gain understanding. I like to keep books and articles on hand for auditory learners and give them time at lunch or during breaks to ask questions. Auditory learners can stump even the most prepared instructors, so keeping up on the latest paddling techniques is essential for their learning.

Poor Jim. He thought he would have fun teaching his kids to paddle and he ended up frustrated; he fell into a classic teacher trap. As I identified, Jim is an auditory learner, and, of course, he is an auditory teacher. Teachers tend to teach to their own learning styles, which can lead to the kind of day Jim had if teacher-student styles do not match up. To make learning experiences student-directed rather than teacher-directed, teachers need to be able to adapt to individual styles, the group's physical and emotional condition, and the prevailing environmental conditions—all of which may change at a moment's notice. If teachers come in with a plan and stick to it without room for unexpected changes, they may be in for a rough and potentially unsafe day. Paddling is more fun when teachers stay alert to the environment and their kids. Discovering the right keys that help kids make connections enhances the wonderful challenge of teaching—the rewards are indescribable.

Some general thoughts about learning:

~ Younger kids learn by making associations, so their early impressions of boats and water must be good ones. If kids associate paddling trips with being cold, hungry, tired, or bored, parents will be hard pressed to get them back on the water.

~ *Spend lots of time swimming so kids are comfortable in the water.*

~ *Resist the temptation to refine techniques until kids are eleven or older or, better yet, wait until they ask for instruction.*

~ *Allow for mistakes and individual choices. Kids learn better if they feel they can make a mistake and still be supported by their peers and teachers. Kids need help developing a transformational attitude about mistakes—parents and instructors have to model this attitude.*

~ *Reinforce curiosity, exploration, and teamwork; kids should feel good about trying new skills. With these conditions in place, kids will develop confidence, judgment, and positive self-esteem.*

~ KEEPING THEM INTERESTED ~

In 1992 we started a summer paddling program at Zoar Outdoor geared toward local kids ages eight through eighteen years old. The purpose of the program was to give the kids some exposure to, and understanding of, the river that flows through their community and to give them something fun to do during summer vacation.

Especially with the younger kids, we play lots of games—the sillier, the better and the quicker they learn. Some days we spend more time out of the boat than we do actually paddling. This is okay; in fact we encourage it since it invisibly builds skills that can be pieced together later. Relay races, switching boats and gear, creating multi-boat flotillas, standing in boats, jumping out of boats, hand paddling, riding on the back or front of another boat, and playing Simon Says, Polo, or Red Light, Green

Light (See Games on page 94) all foster comfort and intimacy with the equipment and the paddling environment.

The first summer Karen taught this age group she had trouble because her expectations were the same as those she had with the adult groups she taught over the years. It quickly became apparent that she was failing at her attempts—the kids were not having fun and she was very frustrated.

One rainy day only a few kids showed up and she had to come up with something fun to do on the spot. On the spur of the moment she announced that they were going to explore an island and look for buried treasure. "Look down the river, see that island? Let's see who can get there the fastest!" she challenged them. And the race was on! Once they all got there, they beached the boats and started exploring the island.

They found all sorts of things: pools of fish, insects, and wetland flowers. The kids were enthralled and Karen was excited to have discovered a teacher's secret weapon—games! The kids said it was the best paddling day so far! They even forgot about the rain and cold. From that point on, Karen overhauled her whole teaching approach with kids and incorporated many games aimed at teaching paddling skills covertly. By the end of the summer she had a pretty accomplished group of little paddlers who were eager to run the easy sections of the river in their kayaks with style and grace!

HOW FAR TO PUSH?

BY JAMIE MCEWAN

I looked back to see if my daughter, Caitlin, was following me; she was, more or less, but instead of tracking my wide loop she was instinctively cutting the corner. Too much?

Looking upstream I could clearly see a wide hole that was no doubt invisible to her from above. I watched her appear briefly as she crested each brown wave of the flooded Housatonic, paddling confidently, a pure and priceless look of exhilaration on her face. And then she hit the edge of the hole, and was over.

"Come on, Caitlin," I muttered under my breath, as her boat's black hull twisted uncertainly in the confused currents of the eddy line. "Come on." Caitlin was thirteen at the time. She had a solid one-hand roll that put my own to shame, but had only rolled a dozen times in rapids, and never in the surging currents of March's cold flood waters. She almost came all of the way up, once, but her slim racing boat was levered back over by a contrary swirl of the eddy line.

And then her head bobbed to the surface. She was out.

When I reached her she had her paddle in one hand, her end loop in the other, just the way I had taught her. Somehow she managed to grab my end loop, too. I looked ahead. The river was wide. The air temperature was below freezing, and the water not much above.

"You can let the boat go!" I shouted to her as I began to paddle for shore.

"No, I've got it," she called in return.

When we finally reached shore I climbed out and emptied her boat while she blew on her hands and held them against her cheeks to warm them while water streamed from her wet gear.

"We're not far from Clarke Outdoors," I told her. "We can jog there in two or three minutes, get warm, catch a ride. Okay?"

"No. I'm all right. Let's keep going."

"Are you sure?"

She was shivering, her face pinched, her hands beet-red and stiff with cold, but she resolutely resisted my continued attempts to convince her to pull out. Why? At first I was puzzled, but later I realized: it was simply because she knew me. It was because no matter what I said, she knew what I really wanted from her, deep down. She had listened to us paddlers tell our macho stories, and she was determined to show that she was just as tough as any of us.

Which she did.

Yes, I know, I should have insisted.

"Keep it fun," everyone says, and it's good advice, as far as it goes. But kids are awfully good at understanding what actors call "sub-text"—the unspoken message that lies behind your words. If you use "keeping it fun" as a technique whose ultimate goal is producing Olympic champions—kids will know what your real goals are.

If they're not your own children, and don't know you well, you might be able to fool them for a while. Or, even if you can't, they may not care about your underlying motivation. (Though you'll have to be a good bit more subtle than one adult whom I watched run down the bank alongside a teen-aged slalom racer, screaming "Relax! Relax!" at the top of his lungs. The kid, with gritted teeth and a death-grip on his paddle, was hearing the sub-text loud and clear.)

In the long run you'll fool nobody. Attitude will always come out. I've finally realized that the most impor-tant step in becoming a good teacher, leader, or parent is *not learning any kind of technique. It's getting your own priorities straight.*

It's not always easy to know what one's own inner motivations really are. Our family, all six of us, takes a yearly camping/canoeing trip in the Adirondacks. Open canoes, loaded with gear, young kids: I knew that our goal was just to be out there. And yet, during the first couple of years, I could not seem to stop myself from being frustrated that we weren't getting off on time in the mornings, weren't knocking off the planned number of miles each day. Only in recent years have I managed to find the appropriate, relaxed rhythm.

Having children is a process of self-discovery. So is teaching.

Too bad the kids have to suffer through our own process of self-discovery.

Caitlin is sixteen now, and much more interested in dancing than paddling, these days. When the weather is good, though, she likes to take an occasional river run. And she asked me along to her school's kayaking club rolling session the other day. Together we taught the class how to get in the boat, wet exit, and roll. Fellow experts, working together.

~ BEING A TEACHER AND A PARENT ~

Teaching your children any kind of skill is one of the most rewarding parts of parenting. Given the general complexity of parent-child relationships, teaching your own children needs to be approached with an extra degree of sensitivity. Kids in general love to learn when learning is synonymous with adventure, exploration, and success. Even young kids can be self-conscious in front of peers and especially in front of their parents. Learning is most successful when your child is drawing knowledge out of you rather than when you are trying to feed it to them. They are often more receptive to being shown rather than told.

Kids will tell you when they are ready to learn, and as a parent, you get to know the signs better than anyone. Our oldest daughter hadn't shown much interest in paddling until one day as I headed off to teach a kayak lesson to some adults, she kissed me goodbye and, out of the blue, asked, "Daddy, could you teach me how to kayak sometime?" I was flabbergasted and when I had regained my ability to speak, I told her, "I would be happy to."

A few weeks later we took an easy raft trip together and a couple of kids followed the rafts in kayaks. When one of them tired of kayaking my daughter couldn't wait to get in and try. She hopped right in, maneuvered unsteadily to where I was sitting on the raft, and asked for some tips on turning the boat. I beamed as I showed her the basics of the sweep stroke and she paddled off downstream diligently practicing what I had taught her.

Frequently children look to a trusted adult other than a parent to teach them something new. Their friend's parent or a close relative often can be more effective than their own parent. Some parents may not have the necessary skills to teach their children, while others may know too much. Rather than seeing it as a bad sign, however, it helps to realize that your kids often have an excellent intuitive sense of whom they can learn from most effectively at a given time and they gravitate toward that teacher.

Let the Motivation Come from the Kids

It's important to let children make their own decisions about whether to take up the sport of paddling. The more committed the parents are to paddling, the more important this is for their children. The feeling that "mom and dad want me to do this" is often enough to turn a child off to paddling for good. Whether parents are paddlers or not, they should offer support and encouragement, not pressure. The same child introduced to paddling through a group of her or his peers might love it.

We teach a program for local children between the ages of eight and eighteen. Some of the kids (often the younger ones) want their parents around during the program. Others' interest waxes and wanes in inverse proportion to the amount of interest their parents show in paddling. They want to find an interest of their own that they can pursue without the pressure, approval or disapproval, and help of their parents. They want to prove to themselves that they can succeed at paddling on their own terms.

∼ LEARNING STYLES VARY WITH AGE ∼

Becky Molina, a mother, an educator, and a paddling instructor on the side, thinks the age at which they are ready to handle their own boat depends greatly on the kid. "I have had success teaching kids as young as six mastery of tandem strokes and maneuvers that allow them safely to navigate a quietly flowing river on a day trip. Our own son will probably develop some abilities sooner than that...as do many children of paddlers. (If they are raised by wolves, they learn early how to hunt. . . .)"

We've heard of kids as young as four years old paddling their own boats through easy rapids or on short flatwater trips. Most camp programs set a minimum age of eight to ten. By that age, many kids are big enough to paddle small adult boats and are strong enough to maneuver against a moderate wind or an easy current. With properly proportioned gear, size and strength shouldn't have to be a major concern in getting kids started.

Twin brothers who tried our local kids program at the age of eight didn't enjoy their first experience. The instructor took a game-oriented but instructional approach. Coming back three years later to the same program, they thrived. Their attention spans were longer, they were bigger, and more able to handle the boats. They were more comfortable on the water and with themselves physically, having participated in school sports in the intervening years.

Kids can start riding in canoes, kayaks, and rafts as young as a few months old. You're not teaching them to paddle at that age, you're simply bringing the baby along while the adults paddle. On the Green River in Utah, we met a family in a canoe with a nine-month-old enjoying the river from under a custom-made sun deck in front of his mom. He was having a great time outdoors with his family.

By taking your kids along, you're showing them the joys of paddling and being outdoors, as well as spending time together as a family. Photo by Ian Ellison.

By two or three years of age, kids can begin to participate in the adventure and enjoy being in a boat for its own sake. Often they like to splash the water with their hands or paddles.

Many rafting companies offer family float trips for kids as young as two or three. This is a great way for kids to get a taste of the excitement paddling can offer without having to pilot their own boats, with mom or dad close by for comfort and safety. One set of parents told us about paddling a double sea kayak with their three-year-old by putting her in the hatch between the two paddlers.

If paddling is something the family does together and with other kids, children are more likely to see it as an enjoyable way to spend time with their parents. If you're into paddling, your children will pick it up; the jargon, the culture, and the equipment, whether you want them to or not.

If you're not a paddler yourself, learning together with children can be a great experience. If you do decide to start out with your children, learning about paddling can be both educational and fun for everyone.

Take them canoe or kayak shopping. Let them help choose destinations or instruction programs you can take together. Don't be surprised if their skills soon outpace yours. Let them enjoy seeing mom and dad taking on something new.

At any age, "teachable moments" occur any time you're on the water with kids. Learning to watch for these moments and to see how children learn spontaneously from them is part of the joy of paddling with kids. But when can you start teaching them strokes, leans, and maneuvers in a more formal sense?

With younger children, it's the whole adventure that counts. The paddling may even be secondary.

The after-school program at Zoar Outdoor began with kids from eight to eighteen years old in the same class, but we found the difference in physical and social ability too great. Ideally, we like to have one session geared for eight- to eleven-year-olds, another for twelve- to fifteen-year-olds, and a third for sixteen- to eighteen-year-olds. Kids in the older groups have started their adolescent growth spurts and have developed some muscle mass. They can carry the boats without assistance, fit better into adult-sized helmets, PFDs, and other gear, and have a bit more endurance than the youngest age group. They also are more focused on learning actual paddling skills and want to head quickly down the river to have fun. One added, unforeseen benefit is that after a child has been in the program a few summers and is old enough (fourteen years and older) to have a good foundation of skills, he or she can assist the younger kids with gear adjustments and simple boat-tow rescues. This gives older children a sense of accomplishment and increases their skills since they are showing others how to do things.

Younger children tend to be more silly and fun loving, but rarely want to learn skills or listen to instructions. Often they need a lot of hand-holding and help with their equipment (this is where the fifteen-year-old assistant really comes in handy). They vie for the instructor's attention with needless requests ("Will you zip my vest?" or "Will you buckle my helmet?") and love to be on center stage ("Look at me I'm in my boat backward!").

A SEVEN-YEAR-OLD PADDLER

BY BRUCE LESSELS

The summer she was seven, our daughter Abbie was ready to try kayaking after watching some other kids a year or two older zip down an easy section of the river. She jumped in a friend's boat and, with a little guidance on how to hold the paddle, was quickly experimenting on her own. The real challenge came when our younger daughter, who was also in a boat, got swept downstream into some branches along the shore. Abbie was able to paddle over to her and bump the boat out of the snag. She was proud to have rescued her little sister and this gave her confidence a huge boost.

Ages Eight through Eleven

Most people agree that it's best to hold off on formal teaching of strokes and maneuvers until kids are at least seven or eight years old. At all ages, but especially for the youngest kids, the main goal should be to ensure that they have fun. Children soak up information. The best thing a teacher, parent, camp counselor, or trip leader can do is to keep the situation safe, relaxed, and fun, and then stand back and let the kids take it all in. Even at this age learning should happen through games and guided discovery, where children are given the proper equipment in a low-risk, safe setting and encouraged to try out strokes or other techniques in a playful manner. Keep the sessions short, and be sure that kids are warm, well fed, and feel secure.

The best teachers for children of any age are other children. Sometimes an older or more experienced friend can act as a motivator for a young child to learn to paddle, and can help guide them in a way that an adult cannot. Let the children learn at their own rate, and realize that they learn best when they are not being "taught" in the sense that we think of teaching to an adult.

An example of this is the way many children learn to feel for resistance with the paddle blade—through splashing each other! After a few hotly contested water battles, they will have learned about the blade angle that sends the most water flying at their friends, and the angle that sends water the farthest at a retreating target.

It's not even necessary that kids spend lots of time in the boats. Part of the attraction to boating is all the time you can spend swimming and splashing. Games that involve paddling on top of an overturned kayak, climbing into a swamped canoe or kayak, or swimming while pulling a boat all promote comfort with the boat and lead quickly to kids learning to wet exit, maneuver the boat, and handle themselves after a capsize. Chapter 6 provides a concise guide to paddling games that develop solid boating skills. On the ocean, kids may spend most of their time wading around a tidal pool searching for starfish. When it comes time to move to the next pool, they may hop in the boats and surprise you with their ability to maneuver along the beach.

At this age, kids are very interested in the world around them and less focused on themselves. This is to their advantage in learning boating, as long as the emphasis is on going someplace, exploring, or learning about the natural world. Kids will pick up the paddling skills tangentially because they are curious and like to experiment. There is no need for sophisticated terminology and drills, since kids learn more by watching and doing at this age. Kayaking also can enhance a kid's self confidence; they are in control of the boat and where they go.

Some kids will ask for instruction at this point and you should give them as much as they want. But don't push it. If you keep it fun, you'll accomplish your goal, and they'll learn far more through their own explorations than you could ever teach them.

Ages Eleven through Fourteen

The huge advantage kids have at this age is body size. Some have had their adolescent growth spurt and are as big as many adults. A bigger body means a stronger body and thus more endurance. Kids can try more challenging and longer paddling trips. They can be in charge of their own gear. They may be more interested in why things occur and how to do things. They want to master certain skills and want more formal instruction. They are curious about learning how to do an Eskimo rescue or how to surf a wave. At this age lots of games, snacks, and swimming are still important, but kids want to paddle on their own and be in more control of their boat.

Games that introduce specific skills and include everyone can create a supportive learning environment. Since kids at this age have the focus and maturity to learn more formally, having a lesson plan is more appropriate than with younger kids. Guidelines, boundaries, and who is in charge need to be established early on for safety reasons, but leave flexibility to adapt to changes in energy levels and water conditions. This is the age where kids can start to take responsibility for themselves and others around them and can choose to participate in activities.

Kids near the older end of this age group can make great teachers. They usually love to help younger kids and are quite good at it. If kids have been paddling for a while, it will really help their own skills to give them leader-ship roles teaching a younger group, while the adult steps back to supervise.

#4: Plan paddling trips and adventures that are appropriate for the age, experience, and ability of the individual child or group.

Ages Fifteen through Eighteen

By high school age, kids can really take off and develop paddling skills at a remarkably fast pace. Motivation is everything at this stage. The kids who love the sport learn through virtually any method. They learn espe-cially well by watching paddlers better than themselves, and some kids find easygoing competition both fun and motivational. The opinions of peers can be particularly important to high schoolers, so maintaining positive peer-group interactions is critical to keeping kids learning. We've seen extremely supportive high schoolers in our after-school program, passing on skills they've learned and helping others to carry their boats and put on their sprayskirts. We've also seen the downside of this sup-port, when one kid feels self conscious because of help from the others. That's when it's time for a game.

Older teenagers often seem to have two modes—disinterested and extremely excited. The more they are challenged, the more excited they become. They are capable of picking up skills at a rapid pace, but only when their interest is piqued. It's not that they don't care about what's going on, so much as they bore easily.

By this age, kids can start taking some real responsibility for the deci-sions involved in paddling. They can help to decide what route to take, whether to attempt a crossing, or whether to continue at all. They should be encouraged to exercise good judgment. The best way for a parent, a trip leader, or an instructor to communicate what is and is not good judg-ment is by making their own decisions clear to the group. Discuss why you decided on a particular route, a particular crossing strategy, or a particular system of group organization. Invite input from the kids.

Misha Golfman is fond of letting kids this age run the day, planning routes, safety setups, and other logistics. The great thing about the outdoors as a hands-on classroom, according to Misha, is that kids "can see the results of their work." If the day runs smoothly, the kids are rewarded with a sense of accomplishment. If things don't go as planned, the feedback is immediate. Of course with safety issues, the school of hard knocks is not always the best place to learn, but the leaders at Kroka Expeditions stay close by in case a situation develops that is beyond the kids' abilities.

CHAPTER FIVE

SKILLS AND STROKES

Starting anyone off in any type of canoe or kayak involves building their skills in a gradual, progressive way. Just as a child must walk before they can run, so anyone new to paddling needs a firm foundation in the basics before taking on more advanced challenges. The following are some methods that we have found particularly effective in presenting the basics to kids. *Remember to adapt these methods to the kids' ages and abilities.*

～ BOAT ENTRIES AND EXITS ～

Getting into and out of the boat is the first thing for a kid to practice and become comfortable with when learning to paddle a canoe or kayak. We generally begin on dry land, then move to the water after the kids have done several successful dry runs. Using this gradual approach minimizes fear and maximizes success. It is good practice to do a short swim test with kids to know how comfortable they are in the water and how they react to cold water.

Before practicing entries and exits, take the time to make the boat fit the child well. Adult-sized boats can be made snugger by duct-taping pieces of foam where the hips meet the sides of the seat, tightening up the back strap and adjusting the foot pedals or bulkhead so their legs fit snugly. Once the boat is wet, duct tape won't stick to it, so do most of the adjusting on dry land before putting boats in the water. Make sure not to put a beginner in a boat that's too snugly outfitted for them. Practice exiting from boats on dry land before heading to the water to ensure that everyone feels comfortable exiting when necessary. Even a boat that feels somewhat snug when upright is usually easy to exit when you're upside down and gravity is on your side.

Entering a kayak can be tricky and it is not uncommon for people to fall into the water as they are trying to get into their boats. Try these strategies for entering a kayak:

~ With a plastic boat that is durable enough to withstand scraping on the shore, enter the boat on dry land near the water. Once you are in your outfitting comfortably, slide the boat into the water, doing a "seal launch."

~ In a less durable boat, turn the boat parallel to shore and use the paddle as an outrigger between the shore and the back of the cockpit rim. With the hand closest to the water, hold both the back of the cockpit and the paddle shaft at the same time. Hold the paddle shaft with the other hand and lean your weight toward the shore, so the paddle blade on shore supports some of your weight. Now step gingerly into the cockpit and slide your legs into the boat. Once you have fully lowered yourself into the seat, remove the paddle from its outrigger position, attach your sprayskirt if you are using one, and paddle away.

Entering a canoe can be just as tricky, although canoes themselves are often more stable than kayaks. To enter a solo canoe, use either the "seal launch" described above for kayaks or:

~ Put the boat in the water parallel to shore.

~ Facing toward the bow, hold onto a gunwale with each hand, crouch low, and put one foot into the center of the boat.

~ Using your hands on the gunwales to balance, stay low and bring the other foot into the boat while sitting down into the seat at the same time.

#5: Always have a fully stocked first-aid kit that is compact and waterproof, and make sure you know how to use it.

To enter a tandem canoe with your partner:

~ Have one partner hold the boat to stabilize it while the other partner gets in.

~ The partner who is getting in first should stay low and climb into their end of the boat.

~ Now the partner who is in the boat can use their paddle to stabilize the boat while the other paddler climbs aboard in the same fashion.

Entering your boat is the hard part. Getting out of your boat when you flip upside down is much easier because gravity is on your side, but it means putting your head underwater, so many paddlers find it scary. Giving kids time to become comfortable with the water makes the whole process much easier for them. Before actually putting the boats into the water, try having the kids float and swim in a calm spot wearing their PFDs. If they are preparing to paddle on whitewater this is a good opportunity to practice the defensive swimming position, lying on their backs with their toes above the surface and their backs arched. They can try rolling like a barrel, diving under water, and bobbing up and down using a scissor kick. This can be done at all age levels—even with adults.

It is best to practice *exiting your boat* on land before trying it in the water. We might have kids race each other getting in and out of their boats on the grass or in sand, where they can flip over and rock their boats side-to-side, learning to control them by moving their hips. These games develop both comfort in the boat and hip and torso control. This is a good time to introduce the concept of tucking their heads forward and kissing the deck in a protective position when they flip over.

The next step is to take the boat into the water without sitting in it. The kids can swim or float next to their boats by holding onto one of the grab loops. They can practice swimming to shore with their boats. Let the kids climb over, under, and into the boats if they wish. It is pretty hard to get into an upright boat from the water. Flip the boats over and have the kids submerge and come up in the air pockets created by the cockpits. This is a pretty cool discovery for most kids—hey, I can breathe under here!

Now try submerging the boat while sitting in it. With the help of assistants, sink each boat with kids sitting in it. Have the kids relax, get out of the boat, and float to the surface. This is as far as you need to go with a canoe unless it is outfitted with thigh straps and a pedestal that can hold a paddler in the boat when they are underwater. With a kayak or a closed canoe, repeat this exercise, this time with sprayskirts. Prior to this, have the kids practice pulling the sprayskirt off on land to be sure they are strong enough to do it.

The next step in a kayak or closed canoe is to roll over and try to hang underwater. For a tentative kid, tip them halfway over into an instructor's arms, so they can get their face wet but are not fully submerged until they are ready. When the student is ready the instructor can gently roll the boat all the way over. Let them hang for a few seconds underwater before the instructor pulls the boat upright by reaching over the hull and rolling the boat up. Eventually the child should be able to hang out underwater until they slap the boat as a signal to be pulled up.

Another method of teaching kids to wet exit a closed boat is to have them get back into the boat while it is upside down. It works best with older kids who have greater lung capacity and more developed muscles. With the boat flipped over, have the student duck under it facing the stern, grab the sides of the boat, and do a backward somersault into the boat. In a kayak this will put the paddler's legs under the front deck and their backside into the seat. In a canoe outfitted for whitewater the drill puts the knees in the knee cups and the backside on the pedestal or seat. Once in position, the boat can be pulled upright or the kid can exit the same way they just entered.

Once a student is comfortable, they can try flipping the boat over themselves and exiting the boat while the instructor stands in the water next to them. The final goal is for the student to do a self-rescue—flip themselves over, hang out underwater for as long as they can, exit the boat without any assistance, and swim their gear to shore.

~ STROKES ~

The strokes used in a canoe, a kayak, or a raft are more similar than different. For the beginner first learning to maneuver a boat on flatwater, the ability to perform a few key strokes well is more important than learning the entire range of strokes. For this reason, we focus on universal strokes used to maneuver a kayak or a canoe on either flatwater or whitewater. For more detail on these strokes and many others, consult one of the references listed in Appendix E.

First a few terms: the *active paddle blade* in a kayak is the one in the water doing the work. This active blade is attached to the active hand, arm, and shoulder. A canoeist's *on side* is the side on which they paddle in a regular forward stroke. A canoeist's *off side* is the side on which they must cross their paddle over the boat in order to take a stroke. Similarly, a canoeist's on-side hand, arm, and shoulder are those on the same side of their body as the side on which they paddle in a regular forward stroke and vice versa.

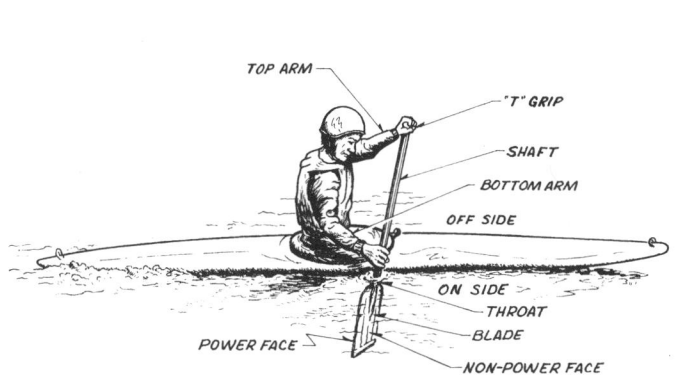

The anatomy of a canoeist and a canoe paddle. Illustration by Noland Hisey.

TOP ARM
"T" GRIP
SHAFT
BOTTOM ARM
OFF SIDE
ON SIDE
THROAT
BLADE
POWER FACE
NON-POWER FACE

~ HOLDING A PADDLE ~

Canoe

Hold the grip of a canoe paddle with your top hand by folding your hand over the grip while hooking your thumb under the space below the grip.

Hold the shaft of the paddle with your bottom hand about one hand's width above the throat of the paddle.

Kayak

Grip the kayak paddle with each hand about a hand's width in from the throat. Kayak paddles are often feathered, meaning both blades are not in the same plane. This is done to minimize wind resistance to the blade in the air and one hand (usually the right hand) is the "control hand." The control hand allows a paddler to know the angle of each blade without looking at the paddle.

To put a right-hand control paddle in the home position, hold the paddle out in front of you with the power face (it will be concave if the blade is curved) of the right blade facing toward you. Note the position of your right hand on the paddle shaft. With oval or "indexed" shafts the long axis of the oval should line up with the crotch of your right thumb.

~ FORWARD STROKE ~

Canoe

The trick to doing the *forward stroke* efficiently is to use as much of the larger back and torso muscles and as little of the arm muscles as possible.

To accomplish this:

~ Think of your upper body as a large rubber band that you first stretch to its maximum length and then release, allowing the energy it has built up to be applied to the paddle.

~ When you place the paddle in the water at the beginning (or catch) phase of the stroke, your bottom arm should be straight and the same shoulder should be pointed at the bow, causing your torso to face away from the side on which you are paddling.

~ Insert the blade into the water by driving down on the grip with your top hand and unwinding your torso so your shoulders end up facing directly forward at the end of the "pull" phase.

~ Your bottom arm should stay straight throughout the stroke so the power generated by your torso is transmitted directly to the paddle through your bones and ligaments and not through the muscles that would be needed to keep the arm bent.

~ To recover, simply drop your top hand to your non-paddle side, bend your bottom arm slightly to lift the paddle out of the water, and return to the catch position.

The catch position for a canoe forward stroke.

Kayak

The *kayak forward stroke* comes naturally once a paddler has mastered feathering the paddle blades by using their control hand to control the blade angles. In a kayak forward stroke each stroke acts as the recovery phase of the stroke preceding it.

~   Extend one arm and shoulder forward toward the bow and place that blade in the water right next to the boat as far forward as you can comfortably reach.

~   Using your torso muscles, pull the active blade toward you until it just about reaches your hips.

~   At that point, lift the active blade out of the water and at the same time place the inactive blade in the water as far forward and as close to the boat as possible.

~   The inactive blade now becomes the active blade and the process repeats itself.

In a *power forward stroke,* work to keep the paddle shaft as vertical as possible when viewed from the front of the boat. This will minimize the amount of turning that the boat will do from side to side as each stroke is applied. For more relaxed paddling over longer stretches, try a touring stroke in which the paddle shaft is more horizontal. This stroke is often used in a sea kayak which, with its pronounced **V** and long hull, has less tendency to yaw from side to side.

In the kayak forward stroke the top hand punches forward at about eye level. As a stroke on one side is finished, you are ready to take a stroke on the other side.

No matter which stroke you are doing, work to use the larger muscles of your torso to generate power for the stroke by rotating your torso from side to side. Point first one shoulder, then the other at the bow as you set up for one stroke and simultaneously recover from the previous one.

~ CORRECTION STROKES ~

The greatest challenge a beginning paddler often faces is making his boat move in a straight line. Each forward stroke turns the boat away from the paddle side, causing it either to wag from side to side, or to veer off course. Canoeists and kayakers have developed strategies known as "correction strokes" for coping with this tendency.

Canoe

A solo canoe paddler has a blade on only one side of the boat. With each forward stroke on that side, the boat not only moves forward, but turns away from the paddle side. This effect is felt even in a tandem canoe, because the stern paddler's forward strokes have more of a turning effect than the bow paddler's strokes.

While there are several ways to correct in a canoe, the two most common are the *pry correction* and the *J stroke*. Both of these corrections are done at the end of a standard forward stroke by either the stern paddler in a tandem canoe or by a solo paddler.

To do a *pry correction*:

~ Turn your top thumb up and toward you at the end of a forward stroke. The blade should now be vertical in the water and nearly flat against the side of the boat just at or behind your hip.

~ Hold the paddle against the side of the boat to steer, as if it were the rudder on a sailboat.

~ When the boat is back on course, pull the paddle out of the water and go on to the next stroke.

This stroke can be made more forceful by pulling in toward the keel of the boat quickly with your top hand just as the blade comes into the pry position.

The *J stroke* is nearly identical to the pry correction except that at the end of the forward stroke the top thumb should point down or away from the paddler. It is important on both the **J** stroke and the pry correction to have the top hand out over the gunwale on the same side of the boat as the bottom hand. This allows the paddle to sit vertically against the side of the boat, providing an angle that maximizes turning and minimizes drag on the boat.

Kayak

In a kayak the forward stroke is symmetrical, because the paddle has a blade on each side. When paddling forward in a kayak, a stroke on the left is usually followed immediately by a stroke on the right. The turning effect of each stroke on the left is offset by the opposite turning effect of each stroke on the right. No paddler has a perfectly symmetrical stroke, so kayakers make course corrections by incorporating subtle sweep strokes into the rhythm of their forward paddling. Some sea kayaks avoid the need for *sweep corrections* by use of a rudder.

Done correctly, sweep corrections are nearly invisible. The paddle shaft goes from vertical on the forward stroke to a bit more horizontal on a sweep correction. To get good at doing this, work on making lots of tiny corrections rather than a few big ones by aiming at a fixed point on shore. When you find yourself deviating even a degree or two, correct immediately.

~ Draw Strokes ~

Canoe and Kayak

The *draw stroke* can cause either a canoe or a kayak to turn or sideslip toward the paddle side of the boat. To pull a solo canoe or kayak sideways with a draw stroke:

~   Rotate your shoulders toward your paddle on the side on which you want to do the stroke (toward the on side in a canoe).

~ Place your active blade in the water with the paddle shaft held vertically so that your top hand is directly over your bottom hand.

~ Reach as far away from the boat as possible by extending your bottom arm and plant the paddle in the water.

~ Draw the paddle directly toward you by driving down with the top hand and pulling in with the bottom hand.

~ To recover, either drop your top hand forward and lift your bottom hand slightly so the blade clears the water, or continue to hold the blade in the water next to the boat where it finished the stroke, turn it ninety degrees, and slice it away from the boat. If the blade is properly angled you should feel minimal resistance to this motion.

In a tandem canoe, if the bow and stern paddlers are paddling on opposite sides of the boat and each performs a draw stroke as described above, the canoe will turn in a circle because the paddlers are located near the ends of the boat.

In a kayak a gliding draw or a duffek acts as a bow rudder to guide your boat around a turn.

To turn a solo canoe or kayak, use a special variation on a draw stroke known as a *gliding draw* or a *duffek*. Either one of these two strokes will guide a turn that has already been initiated by a sweep stroke or by some other method. The gliding draw works best in short, easy-to-turn whitewater playboats, while the duffek works better in longer whitewater or touring boats.

To do a *gliding draw*:

~ Take several strokes forward to give the boat momentum.

~ Place the paddle in the water as described on the previous page under the third bullet.

~ Hold the paddle in this position (without drawing it in toward the boat) and rotate the blade slightly to move its leading edge away from the boat and "open" the blade angle. By varying the angle with which you rotate the blade, you will be able to adjust the amount the boat turns.

~ Note that this stroke only works as long as the boat has momentum.

With a duffek in the bow of a tandem canoe and a forward sweep in the stern, you can set up a powerful turn. Photo by Noland Hisey.

To make a gliding draw into a *duffek*, simply place the paddle in the water farther forward by extending your bottom arm forward and bringing your top forearm across your forehead, as if you were going to read your watch and your eyes were in your forehead.

~ CROSS DRAW STROKE ~

Canoe

The *cross draw stroke* is done only in a solo canoe or in the bow of a tandem canoe. It is very similar to the draw stroke, except that it is done on the paddler's off side. The trick is not changing hands in order to do this stroke. To perform a cross draw:

~ Hold the paddle with a normal grip and lift it up and over the bow of the boat to place it in the water on the off side. It may make this motion easier if you choke up on the shaft a few inches with the bottom hand.

~ The top thumb should be pointed up and the top hand should be next to and at the bottom of your ribcage.

~ Your shoulders should now be facing the off side.

~ Rotate your torso farther to the off side, place the blade in the water as far from the boat as is comfortable, and pull the blade toward the boat by allowing your torso to unwind.

A cross draw in a solo canoe. Photo by Noland Hisey.

~ FORWARD SWEEP STROKE ~

Canoe and Kayak

The *forward sweep stroke* works in either a solo canoe or kayak and a slight variation of it is useful for a stern paddler in a tandem canoe or kayak. It is an aggressive stroke that moves the boat forward while turning it away from the side on which the stroke is done at the same time. The steps for a forward sweep are:

~ Hold the paddle shaft as horizontally as possible by lowering the top hand so it is just above the deck (or the gunwales of an open canoe).

~ Rotate your torso so the on-side or active shoulder faces the bow of the boat while extending the on-side or active arm and blade forward.

~ Place the blade in the water as close to the bow as possible without leaning forward.

~ Keep the on-side or active arm extended and sweep the blade away from the boat in a wide arc, ending just before the blade hits the boat toward the stern. The power for this stroke should come from rotating the torso so that at the end of the stroke your on-side or active shoulder points at the stern.

~ To recover, drop the top hand slightly, lift the bottom hand slightly, and rotate your torso to return to the catch position.

To apply the forward sweep to a paddler in the stern of a tandem canoe or kayak, do only the last half of the stroke by starting at the halfway point—where the paddle is extended at ninety degrees to the boat and the paddler's shoulders are square to the boat. Now continue the sweep toward the stern, ending just before the blade hits the boat.

A forward sweep stroke starts at the bow and describes a wide arc away from the paddler toward the stern.

~ REVERSE SWEEP STROKE ~

Canoe and Kayak

The *reverse sweep stroke* applies in both a canoe and a kayak. This stroke turns the boat powerfully while slowing or stopping its momentum. It is often used to make sharp turns in sea kayaks because of the difficulty of turning against the pronounced **V** in their hulls. As the name implies, the reverse sweep is nothing more than the forward sweep done backwards:

~ Starting with the on-side or active shoulder facing the stern and the paddle extended toward the stern, sweep a wide arc toward the bow using the rotation of your torso to generate power for the stroke.

~ End the stroke just before the paddle hits the bow.

As with the forward sweep, stern paddlers in a tandem boat often do part of the reverse sweep. In this case, they do the first half, starting with the paddle at the stern and ending the stroke when the paddle is perpendicular to the boat and opposite their hips.

~ HIGH AND LOW BRACES ~

Canoe and Kayak

A brace can prevent a boat from flipping if done at the right moment and with enough commitment. The principle of a brace is simple: place the blade flat on the water and use its resistance to support your body weight and to bring the boat back upright after a near upset. It takes a lot of work to turn a brace into a reflex, but kids love to get wet, so bracing practice on a warm summer day can be great fun.

The position of the paddler's elbows relative to their hands is what determines whether a brace is a *high brace* or a *low brace*. Hands above elbows is a high brace, while hands below elbows is a low brace.

A high brace in a kayak—note that the paddler is dropping his head down while righting the boat with his hips.

The steps for a *high brace* are:

~ Hold the paddle with your arms straight out in front of you, as if you were checking your grip for home position in a kayak.

~ Bend both elbows so the paddle comes toward your chest.

~ Be sure the active blade is parallel to the water so the blade will have maximum resistance to the downward pressure you will apply.

~ Extend the blade toward your on side (the active side in a kayak) and place the blade on the water.

~ The next three steps happen nearly simultaneously. Lean over toward the paddle with your boat and your body, then throw your head down toward the paddle while righting your boat with your hips, knees, and legs.

~ When the boat is stable under you, sit up again.

~ The last thing to come out of the water should be your head.

The steps for a *low brace* are similar to the high brace:

~ Again, hold the paddle with your arms straight out in front of you. The blade (the active blade in a kayak) should be facing back toward you.

~ Drop your hands, rotating your elbows up and your hands down, so they are directly below your elbows. At the same time extend the paddle out toward your on side (your active side in a kayak) with the blade flat on the water.

~ In a canoe, reach your top hand out over the gunwale so it touches the water before your bottom hand. In a kayak, simply keep your non-active hand just above the deck of the boat and your active hand out over the water on your active side.

Starting a low brace in a closed canoe. Note that the T-grip hand is lower than the shaft hand at the beginning of the brace.

The last part of the low brace is the same as the high brace:

~ The next three steps happen nearly simultaneously. Lean over toward the paddle with your boat and your body, then throw your head down toward the paddle while righting your boat with your hips, knees, and legs.

~ Finally, when the boat is stable under you, sit up again.

~ The last thing to come out of the water should be your head.

The low brace is commonly used in a canoe; the high brace is commonly used in a kayak. The presence of the second blade in a kayak prevents the paddler from extending his top hand out over the side of the boat to position the blade properly on the water.

~ ESKIMO ROLL ~

Canoe and Kayak

Both canoeists and kayakers can learn to *Eskimo roll* if they have a boat with proper outfitting. For a canoe the boat must have at least thigh straps to hold the paddler in when they are upside down, and a significant part of the inside of the canoe must be filled with flotation bags—large vinyl or nylon air bladders that displace water and keep the boat from filling completely when tipped over. To roll a kayak the paddler needs thigh hooks, foot braces, and a snug enough seat that they can readily control the lean of the boat with their hips and legs. In addition, a kayak must have a cockpit that can accept a sprayskirt to keep water from entering the boat when upside down.

The principle of the Eskimo roll is similar to that of a brace. The trick is that the whole thing is performed underwater. It is beyond the scope of this book to go into much detail on the roll. The following photo sequence demonstrates the Eskimo roll in both a canoe and a kayak. See Appendix E for more information on the Eskimo roll.

The sequence of motions needed to perform an Eskimo roll in a kayak (Photos courtesy of Susan Connolly):

The set up with head tucked.

The set up position just after flipping.

Sweeping out to ninety degrees.

The hip snap—note that the head comes out of the water last.

The sequence needed to perform an Eskimo roll in a canoe (Photos courtesy of Susan Connolly):

CHAPTER SIX

GAMES AND OTHER WAYS TO REACH KIDS

~ TEACHING STROKES AND MANEUVERS TO KIDS ~

The basic forward, sweep, and draw strokes are generally easy to teach to kids and many of the principles apply equally to kayaks and canoes. Children often figure out these strokes just by experimenting with the paddle. With some encouragement they can learn to make their sweeps extend far away from the boat for maximum turning power, and to keep their forward strokes right next to the boat to avoid turning. They can learn to keep their top hand directly over their bottom hand during a draw by thinking of their top hand as arching over their head as a ballerina's does when she twirls. They can learn to involve their torsos in all three strokes by watching another paddler demonstrate the correct technique.

Reverse strokes come even more naturally, and you may find yourself trying to discourage their overuse rather than encouraging good technique. The concepts of boat leans, body leans, and braces are best taught on a warm flat lake or in a pool.

Before proceeding to moving water or to large bodies of open water, kids should be completely self-sufficient with wet exits and self rescues. Dry-land exercises should cover safe river-running practices, rescue techniques, and river or ocean features as appropriate. These exercises can employ videos, chalkboard talks, or items from nature to create a model river or a make-believe lake or ocean scenario.

After giving a basic river or ocean talk, try having the kids divide up into smaller groups and create their own paddling setting using natural props such as sticks, stones, grass, sand, shells, or whatever they find in their surroundings. By creating a paddling setting, they demonstrate an understanding of the dynamics of the setting. In a classroom, they can create more abstract props using colored paper, markers, string, and recyclables.

Kids often learn most quickly through hands-on instruction.

Stroke Practice

by Bruce Lessels

Ken Stone has taught kids extracurricular paddling after school for more than twenty years. He focuses on strokes as the basis for both flatwater and whitewater maneuvers: "I have found that skill instruction works best when broken down into individual strokes: forward, reverse, duffek, sweep, and then combination strokes like duffek into a forward stroke or duffek to sweep. We emphasize boat control using strokes and paddle placement, and we begin every practice with twenty minutes of stroke drills on flat water. Novice boaters spend a full two weeks on flat water, practicing strokes and boat control, before we attempt a Class I moving-water descent. As soon as we graduate to moving water we begin by defining the features of whitewater like eddies, wave trains, current differentials, rocks, and the like. We start to practice eddy turns, peel outs, and ferries, both front and reverse. The moves, such as an eddy turn, are broken down into the sequence of strokes that will best result in the proper turn. A left eddy turn might be something like a stroke sequence of left forward, right forward, left forward, right sweep, left duffek, right sweep, left forward."

Circle Paddling

Circle paddling is a popular teaching technique for both kids and adults. It provides a simple conceptual framework common to kayaks and canoes—every maneuver is described in terms of arcs of a larger or smaller circle.

To get started in circle paddling, have the group form a big circle with plenty of room between boats, and paddle clockwise. The instructor slowly closes the circle until the boats are almost touching end to end. Then the group turns around and paddles counter clockwise. By varying the size of the circle, kids learn to make course corrections that help them paddle in a straight line. You also can have them practice leaning the boat to the inside of the turn. When the circle is fairly small, try having everyone paddle only on the inside of the turn and then only on the outside of the turn. Have them compare the effect on their boats. Kids who have mastered making controlled circles going forward can try paddling in a circle backwards. Move the circle to a wide eddy on an easy current and kids are doing peel outs and eddy turns without labeling them as such. The possibilities are as endless as a circle.

Circle paddling helps kids learn to turn without a lot of explanation.

~ GAMES ~

It's remarkable how many silly things you can do in a kayak or a canoe. Playing in boats offers a great way for kids to learn and practice paddling skills all in the name of fun. Games can be incorporated into a lesson at any age or skill level. Paddling lessons usually start off on calm water like a pond or lake where games reinforce basic skills. Remember that in order to enjoy many of these games, kids first need some basic skills instruction.

When introducing a game, be clear and concise in your instructions; *make sure safety is a top priority* and that the kids are having fun. A game that is appropriate for eight- to ten-year-olds may be boring for a teenager, although most games are easily modified to suit different ages. Another consideration is cooperative versus competitive games. At older ages competitive races are more appealing to kids than cooperative approaches. At younger ages, races can be frustrating and result in kids quitting, crying, or being isolated from the activity. The following are some games suitable for any type of boat.

Flatwater Games

Playing games on flatwater is a great way to introduce kids to paddling equipment and to start to give them a sense of how their boat will respond in various situations. Through the use of games, you can reinforce specific skills that have been taught in a more formal way. Kids will naturally figure out many ways to move the boat. By circulating around the class during a game and offering individualized pointers, you can nudge kids in the right direction, while helping those who might not come up with a certain technique for moving the boat on their own. Many of these games may result in kids tipping over, so they need to be comfortable exiting their boats if necessary. Our rule for all games is that when someone flips over, either the game stops until they are back in their boat, or the person who flipped and anyone helping them recover is immune from being tagged, splashed, or whatever else the game calls for until the paddler who flipped is back in their boat and ready to play again.

Games reinforce paddling skills and give kids confidence in a boat.

Sharks and Minnows:

This is one of our favorites. It is a variation on tag in which one person starts out as the shark while everyone else is a minnow. Since sharks eat minnows for lunch . . . you get the picture.

The shark tags a minnow who then becomes a shark and tries to tag other minnows. Eventually, there are lots of sharks and only one minnow paddling for his life. There are pre-established boundaries and only boat-to-boat tags are allowed. You also can limit tagging to bow-to-stern only, or you can allow hand-to-boat tagging, but the idea is to avoid tagging with the paddle so kids aren't swinging them around like war clubs.

Another variation of this game is *Good and Evil*. Half the group starts off being good and half starts off being evil. Each side tries to convert the other by tagging them. In Good and Evil you have to specify bow-to-stern tags only, otherwise each time a boat touches another, the answer to the question, "Who tagged whom?" is ambiguous. The game ends when everyone is either good or evil.

POY/YOP:

This is another version of tag introduced to us by a Zoar Outdoor instructor who spent time paddling in Ireland. One paddler is "it" and tries to tag (hand-to-bow) everyone else. Once tagged, a paddler is "frozen," raises her paddle in the air, and says *POY, POY, POY* continuously until someone who is not "it" unfreezes her by tagging her hand-to-bow. The game ends when everyone except the person who is "it" is frozen. The YOP part of the game is the reverse of POY—everyone paddles backwards and the person who is "it" must tag the stern of each person's boat. Any paddler who is frozen says *YOP, YOP, YOP* until they are unfrozen.

Ultimate Sponge/Dead Fish Polo:

This is ultimate frisbee with a large colorful sponge (the dead fish). Divide the group into evenly skilled teams and set boundaries and goals. Paddling with the sponge in your boat is not allowed—it is the equivalent of traveling in basketball. You can pass the sponge with your hands or paddle. This game can also be played with a lightweight beach ball or an empty milk jug with an airtight top. To add variety put more than one sponge or ball into the game!

Simon Says:

This traditional game can be a great skill enhancer and is especially popular among younger kids. One person is selected to be Simon. Simon can say just about anything—"get out of your boat," "paddle backwards," "link arms with the nearest person," "trade boats with another paddler," "paddle with your hands while lying on top of your boat" —almost anything goes with this game.

Red Light, Green Light:

Another old-time favorite landlubber game is great on the water. This game practices stopping on a dime, starting, and backing up quickly—skills that are important anywhere kids paddle.

Start with all the paddlers except one, "the traffic controller," lined up abreast of each other. The traffic controller paddles a short distance away from the others and faces away from them. The traffic controller then calls out "green light!" signaling the paddlers to sprint toward the traffic controller. At his whim, the traffic controller calls out "red light!" signaling them to stop. The traffic controller immediately turns around to look over his shoulder at the other paddlers. Anyone caught still paddling (or not stopping their boat abruptly, depending on the skill of the group) by the traffic controller is sent back to the starting line again. The game ends when the first paddler tags the traffic controller's boat bow-to-stern.

Mother May I?:

Younger kids often enjoy the water-based version of this popular game. The "mother" starts out about 50 to 100 feet away from the other players. Each player in their turn asks "Mother may I take one baby stroke?" (or giant stroke or any other silly kind of stroke you can think of). The mother replies according to her whim, either "Yes you may," "No you may not," or "No, you may take one backstroke" (or any other stroke she can think of). The first paddler to touch the mother's boat wins. Spice things up by having kids ask if they may take a certain number of a given stroke such as a forward stroke, sweep stroke, or back stroke.

Paddling Patterns:

A great way to work on boat control is to challenge kids to paddle in a square, circle, triangle, or any other shape. In trying to make a given shape, they are fine-tuning their maneuvering abilities and figuring out which strokes move their boats most effectively.

Give Me:

Karen has used this game with great success when teaching kids how to cross-country ski. It is equally fun on the water. The instructor is at the finish line about 100 feet away from the group. The kids divide into two or more teams. At the instructor's signal, a paddler from each team races toward the instructor using the technique and equipment designated by the instructor. The instructor may say, for example, "Give me someone paddling backwards wearing two helmets;" or she may request two paddlers moving together without using paddles, or two paddlers using only one boat or any other silly variation. The first team across the finish line wins. The game can be spiced up by providing a box of props like silly hats, colorful costumes, or items to balance on the deck of the boat.

Piano Keys:

Line up all the boats in the water facing in the same direction. Each person holds on to the boat next to her to keep the boats in line (paddles are left on shore). The paddler at one end climbs out of her boat and tries to walk from her end to the other and back on the lined-up boats without falling in. Of course, the boats are not a stable platform, so expect lots of kids to end up in the water. If older kids find this game too easy, have them try walking backwards or closing their eyes to increase the challenge.

Relay Races:

This is a game better suited for older, more competitive kids. Divide into two teams and arrange all the gear on shore. Everyone starts off wearing only shorts, T-shirts, PFDs, footwear, and whatever warm clothing the conditions require. The gear on shore includes helmets, sprayskirts, paddles, and boats. The first team member races to put on their helmet and sprayskirt (if necessary), picks up their paddle, and paddles to a designated point and back. When they return, they take off their gear and tag the next team member. Each team member follows the same routine until everyone has had a turn. Keep PFDs on throughout the game as a safety precaution, since the action takes place near the water.

Simple relay races that don't involve putting on and taking off gear also work well. If your group is more advanced, try racing backwards.

Another way to play is to have paddlers carry an item over and back from the shore. Try a big beach ball on your deck, paddle using only your hands or ping-pong paddles, or balance a frisbee on your helmet!

Personal Bests:

With groups of varying skill levels, where you may not want to encourage competition among the group, try having kids establish and work to beat their own personal performance standards. This allows each paddler to focus on their own skills rather than on beating the group.

The instructor can introduce a skill, demonstrate the proper way to do it, and then allow time for the kids to practice. The skill can be as easy as paddling forward in a straight line or turning through obstacles (anchored milk jugs or natural rocks) in the water. Have the kids keep track of how many milk jugs or rocks they hit each time and work to reduce this number to zero.

Another way to work with personal bests is to have each paddler spin their boat and count the number of strokes needed to complete a 360. Each time around, the paddlers try to reduce the number of strokes it takes to complete a full turn. This is a great, fun way to develop effective sweep strokes.

Follow the Leader:

At first the instructor is the leader and paddles a course that uses all the skills the group has worked on to this point. Be sure to leave sufficient distance between boats. This is not a race, but rather a chance for kids to practice their skills. After the instructor has led for a while, each kid takes a turn being the leader, showing off her new skills.

More Advanced Games

Once kids feel totally at home on flatwater, they are ready to move to a mild river setting or a large body of water with gentle waves and wind. Current, wind, and waves make a boat handle differently than on flatwater, and strokes must be executed with more confidence and precision. Kids get this difference intuitively, but younger ones may not have the strength to match the power of the water. When playing games on this kind of water, the instructor needs to take these strength differences into account.

Follow the Leader:

In this variation, the leader can use natural features such as waves, wind, shoreline characteristics, eddies, and currents to set a course. The rules are the same as those described above. Participants may get pushed off-line by the wind, waves, or current and involuntarily fall behind, but the desire to keep up forces kids to use strokes more effectively, making their boats go in the right direction. There's no sitting back and floating in this version.

Beat the Clock:

This game works on peel outs and ferries in current. Start in a big eddy on one side of the river. Have a student point the bow of his boat directly upstream in the eddy. His bow is now pointed to twelve o'clock. Eleven o'clock is slightly left of this heading; one o'clock is slightly right of it. Six o'clock is directly downstream.

Now have the student paddle out of the eddy with his boat pointed at nine o'clock, if the eddy he is in is on river left (three o'clock if it's on river right). What happens? Next, have him try it at ten o'clock (or two o'clock on river right), then at eleven (or one). The goal is to ferry without peeling out and to help kids learn to find the ideal ferry angle for each particular site.

Scavenger Hunt:

This game works in almost any location where a variety of natural treasures can be found. Divide the kids into small groups of two to four boats each and give each group a list (the lists can all be the same or different). With younger kids, you may want an adult to accompany each group. Older kids can go out on their own within predetermined boundaries. This game takes the focus off paddling skills and puts it on teamwork, getting places, and learning about nature. Kids love working together and in the long run their paddling improves. Objects to find can be as simple as a rock, a leaf, a clam shell, a gull feather, or a bottle cap. To add a nature-studies component to this game, have the kids identify the items in their collections at the end of the game and how they fit into the local environment.

Slalom Gates:

Whitewater slalom racing is much like ski slalom. The competitors weave in and out of gates, poles hanging from wires suspended between trees above a rapid, trying for the fastest time without hitting any of the gates. The lessons learned from slalom racing apply to any area of paddling, so many paddlers who are not serious slalomists paddle gates to improve their precision and stroke timing. Slalom gates offer a great way for kids to play games such as follow the leader and relay races.

Slalom gates can be hung on almost any pond or river. In shallow water, inflated milk jugs anchored in place about five to six feet apart work well and are easy to set up. On a faster-moving river, more traditional gates with round wooden poles suspended from trees that reach across the river may be the only option. The paddler moves through and around the gates in a predetermined pattern, trying not to hit any. Start off with a few gates and let the kids play around them before trying to time any runs. The ultimate goal is to run the course cleanly—without hitting any gates and in the fastest time possible.

Slalom gates are a great way to hone skills and develop precision while having fun.

For more complexity, add more gates and make the moves harder. Set a ten-gate course with the stipulation that the paddlers must pass through half the gates in one direction (downstream) and the other half in the other direction (upstream), or add a few gates that paddlers must execute backwards. Try running the course in teams of three boats. The three paddlers have to time their own strokes to avoid hitting the gates, and be aware of where their teammates are on the course so they don't run them over.

#6: Check equipment and gear each time you paddle and always carry a spare paddle.

A site with well-defined features such as rocks, eddies, and jets of current works well for older kids who have mastered the necessary skills and are looking for something challenging. The great thing about gates is that a simple stretch of river becomes more difficult by requiring precision.

These are just a few games that we have found to be popular with kids. Needless to say, you can think up infinite variations and new games on your own—there are no hard and fast rules. The more creative or outrageous the variations are, the better time everyone has. Since kids learn best through play and self-discovery, let them be as silly as they want; rest assured, they are learning whenever and however they are paddling.

CHAPTER SEVEN

PADDLING PROGRAMS FOR KIDS

As paddling has entered the recreational mainstream in the past decade, the number and types of paddling programs available for kids have increased exponentially. For our purposes, we break these programs down into five categories: *school-based, camp-based, community-based, club-based,* and *outfitter-based.* Of course, this is not to downplay the importance of kids learning from parents or other family members, but this type of learning tends to be less structured and more spontaneous.

~ School Programs ~

School-based paddling programs often are started by a staff member or parent who is an avid boater, offering lessons as an alternative to other sports or as a club. Many private schools now consider their paddling and outdoor programs essential tools for attracting top-quality students.

One great advantage of learning to paddle as a school sport is that kids can take it gradually, learning a new skill or two each day in the one- to two-hour time slot allotted to athletics. The disadvantage of learning in school is that unless parents are into the sport, the need to buy a boat and other paddling gear and to have a vehicle to transport boats to a lake or river results in many kids giving up paddling after they graduate.

School programs can be recreational or competitive in their focus. Several successful whitewater racing programs are based at private schools around the country, and an equal number of programs focus on recreational paddling. Most of these programs are started and taught by a dedicated individual whose own paddling focus often dictates the focus of the program.

RUNNING A SUCCESSFUL SCHOOL PADDLING PROGRAM

BY KEN STONE

I would strongly recommend that any "start-up" paddling program consider calling itself a racing program rather than a recreational program. I have run both. The advantage of having a racing program is you are able to concentrate more on skills; the novice paddler learns quickly and becomes a competent boater much sooner. In a recreational program the emphasis is not usually on skills and boat control, but rather on the enjoyment of river running.

Four factors are necessary for a successful secondary school paddling program: a competent leader, a willing school administration, a reasonable training/practice site, and adequate equipment.

Since paddling is often a minor school sport, the leader is the most important of the four factors and he must wear many hats. In most programs, the leader is the motivator, the organizer, the fund-raiser, the coach, and the safety instructor. To be successful, the leader must have paddling skills commensurate with the degree of difficulty of the water that will be paddled during the season. I have seen coaches with intermediate skills run successful novice and intermediate programs.

The leader must have knowledge of and experience in all aspects of paddling safety and rescue techniques. Since some degree of danger is always present in paddle sports, safety is of primary importance. Safety begins by knowing the level of your boaters and introducing them to water that challenges them but is not above their level of competence. Safety is the second reason I would choose a racing program over a recreational program. The leader can choose to have the students compete at novice, intermediate, or expert levels and the slalom gates are placed always in the safest, most navigable places on the river. As part of the safety program, hold a mandatory swim test and several pool sessions, to teach and practice wet exits and Eskimo rolls. River signals, self-rescue, and assisted rescue procedures also should be taught on moving water and reviewed periodically until all students are comfortable with the safety procedures.

A sympathetic school administration needs only to grant permission and supply insurance coverage for the program. For public school or private day school programs usually no school transportation is necessary, as parents and the paddlers themselves provide transportation to the training site and races. For private boarding school programs, the school must be willing to underwrite the transportation costs for boaters and for the equipment, which may mean a trailer for the boats. I have run successful paddling programs at two different boarding schools. Both administrations considered the benefits of having such a unique sport as part of the regular athletic program greater than the costs. The schools found that the cost per student was far less than other more traditional sports programs; they did not have to provide equipment, including boats (students purchased their own boats from our stock of inexpensive used boats), pay for uniforms, or underwrite the cost of any type of officiating.

An adequate training site usually means having access to flat water, and Class I or Class II water with training gates hung over the river. Class I training gates are sufficient for a novice or intermediate program. Often the leader can dovetail her efforts to establish and maintain the training site with local paddling clubs. It is extremely important to obtain all proper permissions for river access from landowners and to establish a working relationship with other river users such as anglers, rafters, tubers, or commercial river users.

The cost of equipment is seldom a limiting factor in a student's decision to become a boater. I use a combination of school and individually owned paddling gear, including boats. Because of the high cost of new equipment and the wear and tear caused by first-year paddlers, we outfit our novice boaters with used boats and gear. The additional advantage is if the boater decides not to continue with the sport, we haven't invested much and it is easier to sell the equipment. As the paddlers' skill develops and he wishes to progress to better equipment we can always find a buyer for his used boat and paddling gear. In addition, I have noticed that used boats and paddles often are donated to established programs and can be used for new paddlers with limited funds.

After-school paddling programs provide an alternative to traditional sports. Photo courtesy of Zoar Outdoor.

~ CAMP PROGRAMS ~

It used to be that everyone learned a little bit about canoeing at camp. Skills were passed down from one generation of counselors to the next without incorporating the advances in technique and equipment taking place in the broader paddling world. With the rise of specialty camps over the past few decades, several programs now offer cutting-edge paddling instruction, leading the development of new techniques and equipment.

CAMP MONDAMIN'S PHILOSOPHY

BY FRANK BELL JR.

At our summer camp, Camp Mondamin in North Carolina, we have found paddling to be a perennial favorite activity. While there's much to learn about a canoe or a kayak, a youngster can have fun at any skill level. In a short time, he can learn basic safety (including a surprise flip), enough nomen-clature to call a paddle a paddle (not an oar!), and a few basic strokes. Before too long, he can do a pry in the stern to keep the boat straight, work on a J stroke, and turn his boat through an obstacle course. A new world has opened up to him.

Being a bit traditional, we insist that a camper learn good canoeing skills before getting into a kayak. With the potential reward of a trip on a wilderness lake, or better yet the excitement of paddling whitewater, we find many youngsters eager to get started. A problem may arise when the beginning paddler discovers there's more to paddling than was first apparent—the youngster with a less-devel-oped work ethic and the younger child who doesn't under-stand delayed gratification may not have the will to stick with it. This, of course, is where creative teaching is called for: what can we do to reward and encourage kids at the early stages of learning, so they won't give up?

Games, of course, work well; playing in overturned canoes, "swamp wars," and other well-supervised activi-ties break up the hard work. Mixing in some kayak time is also a fine idea. We want campers to learn to paddle a canoe first, but that doesn't mean variety isn't a good idea. Where a full-sized canoe is sixteen feet long and weighs forty-five to seventy pounds, a kid-sized kayak is half as long and half as heavy. The paddler sits at water level, so she doesn't really need a paddle. We play innumerable games, and learning to roll is the highlight of many a young paddler's beginning career.

Once a kid is past the beginning stages and has expe-rienced a canoe camping trip and/or a beginning river trip, he is usually hooked. From there on, it's a matter of refining the strokes and teaching him to recognize and deal with the dangers present on whitewater rivers.

Learning to paddle presents many valuable lessons that adults may need but children seem more ready to learn. Teamwork is important in tandem canoe paddling and becomes even more important on rivers. Even when each person is paddling a solo canoe or kayak, mutual support and cooperation on a river are vital to the safety of the group. Working together, the self-confidence and self-esteem of the teenager is given a boost at the conclusion of her first successful run of Nantahala Falls—a Class III rapid near the camp.

Both boys and girls make superb paddlers. We find that boys consistently overestimate their ability, while girls tend to underestimate their skills. Skilled paddlers who paddle together are likely to develop respect for each other on an entirely new level, regardless of gender.

Of course, paddling isn't for everyone. My daughter is a natural—learning a kayak roll in one session and a hands-only roll in about five minutes. But if it doesn't have four legs, a mane, and a tail, she's not interested. Oh well, horses are great, too, and she's a terrific rider—but that's another story.

~ COMMUNITY PROGRAMS ~

As towns search for ways to keep kids off the streets during summer vacation, community-based paddling programs have grown in popularity. Often grant-funded with a minimal fee for participation, these programs can vary tremendously in their formats, philosophies, and goals.

Kroka Expeditions runs a small but intense program in southern Vermont. Director Misha Golfman looks for kids who really want to take the sport seriously and develop a strong base of fundamental skills. He tells the eleven- to sixteen-year-old kids that the program is not a social club and that he expects them to adhere to high standards for personal behavior and effort. He finds that kids who stick with his program develop first-rate skills in a short time. "A couple of them are better paddlers than I am now," says Misha, who sees the children's progress as a testament to the success of the program.

YOUTH KAYAKING IN DURANGO, COLORADO

BY KENT FORD

Four Corners Riversports Youth Kayaking Program in Durango, Colorado, has been teaching kids for ten years, and has proven to be one of the most successful kids' paddling schools in the country. More than a hundred kids a year go through the program that is co-produced with the City of Durango Parks and Recreation Department.

A big pitch for the program is the concept of lifetime sports. Paddling is a sport that youngsters can continue well past their school years. Parents grasp the idea that a few lessons can help get their kids started with a solid foundation of skills, and they like a program that emphasizes safety and fun.

With the Animas River running right through town, many of the kids' parents are paddlers themselves. The town is well known as an outdoor-sports mecca, with world class mountain biking, skiing, and kayaking. Many kids in the paddling program also take part in the cross-country skiing club.

Durango, Colorado, is perhaps a unique community. Durango has a downtown whitewater park constructed by the City of Durango with the help of thousands of hours of volunteer labor and numerous community donations. Whitewater Park has played host to kayakers and river rafters from around the world. This slalom course has hosted major national and international events, including the Champion International Whitewater Series, and United States Olympic Trials qualifying events. Smelter Rapid has provided the highlight for thousands of recreational kayakers and rafters enjoying the Animas River corridor through town.

Four Corners offers a program for kids who want to get a taste of kayaking. The class takes place on a lake, pool, or moving-water section of the Animas River. The beginning young adult kayaking class is for those who want to get into paddling. This class begins in a lake and a pool, and eventually progresses to various whitewater sections on the Animas River. Advanced kids' programs start on the Animas. Most of the classes are geared for local kids, but the format of one- or two-week classes also makes them ideal for parents who want a fun stop on a southwestern vacation.

~ CLUB PROGRAMS ~

Paddling clubs around the country are starting kids' programs to allow adult members to share the sport they love with their children. By bringing the kids together to focus on paddling, they develop more quickly as paddlers and form friendships with others in the club. Don't be surprised when the kids' paddling skills exceed those of the adults.

The Housatonic Area Canoe and Kayak Squad, or HACKS, started a program in northwestern Connecticut in the mid-1980s called Half-HACKS. Half-HACKS involves young children in paddling and club activities. The program starts off in a pool with games that develop comfort in boats and underwater, and get kids used to the equipment. Eventually the sessions lead to short, easy river trips. The kids paddle downstream with the current on easy Class I to II whitewater where little maneuvering is required. When kids graduate from the program after a few years, they enter 3/4-HACKS, a program for teens. This program focuses more on technique building and river-running skills. Kids are taken on local rivers, compete in easy slalom races, and spend more time paddling with the adults in the club. Many 1/2-HACKS and 3/4-HACKS graduates have become adult club members who compete regularly in regional races, go on club-sponsored river trips, and help with the younger kids.

The HACKS kids' programs succeed because of sustained adult participation and supervision. Other kids' paddling programs have failed because the parents do not stay involved once their kids are finished with the program. Max Wellhouse, a paddler, father, and active member in his Arkansas-based whitewater paddling club, believes that a successful kids' paddling program must have the support of other adults from the club. His club sees mostly the children of adult members participating in the kids' events. According to Max, some of the obstacles for paddling clubs include finding affordable used equipment, liability, and parental involvement. Often a club can hook up with a local outfitter to rent paddling gear at a reduced rate. "You really need to cultivate paddling for kids before they are twelve years of age. Past twelve years, many kids are already invested in what they like to do sportwise," states Wellhouse. The HACKS club is successful in part because the adult members remain active with the kids' programs, even those adults who have no kids participating.

Another issue of club-based programs is the level of instruction. If the club is lucky enough to have top-level paddlers or certified instructors, then participating kids will get good advice and technique. If, however, the club consists of adult paddlers who are beginners themselves, then instruction needs to come from outside the club. As Max observes, "Many adult paddlers do not feel comfortable teaching young kids." Since his paddling club has many long-time paddlers and instructors, it is able to offer instruction clinics for kids. Through the clinics other adult members serve as mentors and give kids the basics they need to get paddling. Check out the local clubs in your area, ask about how they handle teaching new kids, liability, gear, and chaperones. This is especially important if you are not planning to get involved in the club directly by becoming a member and a paddler. In other words, do your homework.

~ OUTFITTER PROGRAMS ~

Since large numbers of adventure-based outfitters discovered the family market in the 1990s, the number of canoe and kayak clinics offered for kids and families has skyrocketed. These clinics tend to be skill-based, short, and intense. Two to five days is a typical duration and the instructors are often top-notch. However, their main expertise may lie in teaching adults, so some clinics may be too intense for younger kids or those who are tentative about paddling.

Outfitter programs are great for introducing kids to the sport. Photo by Ian Ellison.

Some examples of programs offered by outfitters include a three-day Teen Sea Kayak Expedition Camp offered for ages thirteen to sixteen off the coast of Maine, a four-day Kids' Whitewater Kayaking Camp open to kids twelve to fifteen years of age in the Smoky Mountains of North Carolina, and a five-day Mother-Daughter wilderness canoe trip in the Boundary Waters Canoe Area in northern Minnesota.

#7: Be on the lookout for hypothermia—stay warm and dry. Wear appropriate clothing (avoid cotton) and prepare for changes in the weather or a boat capsizing, and bring extra clothes and rain gear.

~ SELECTING THE RIGHT PROGRAM FOR YOUR CHILD ~

One of our jobs as parents is to do everything possible to ensure our children's safety. Children learn best when they are challenged; however, challenge usually involves risk. At Kroka Expeditions, the trip leaders often put the kids in charge for a day. The kids plan the route, prepare equipment and safety items, and run the trip for the entire day. The leaders hang back within reach, but far enough away to let the kids make their own decisions and learn from their own experiences.

This kind of controlled risk-taking is very different than an outfitter or camp that puts kids on the water without appropriate equipment or leadership. Of course, even a well-run program may exceed the level of risk you feel is appropriate for your child. It is important to understand, however, that every human activity carries risks.

Without solid statistics on every activity and for every organization, evaluating the risks of a paddling program for your kids can be difficult. The best programs, however, are happy to share information about their past safety record, the qualifications of their staff, and their planned itineraries, backup plans, and evacuation procedures. Strong programs see this as a chance to crow about their assets. Weak programs may find this sort of probing threatening.

So what should you look for in a program? The following is a list of questions that you can ask a paddling program to help you evaluate the risks your child may encounter:

~ *What is your safety record?* Get a sense of how many accidents/ injuries the organization has had in the past several years and how many total guests they have taken on trips. If there have been any major incidents, find out what the organization's response was to these incidents.

~ *What are your staff's qualifications?* American Canoe Association (ACA) certification is the standard for instructors in any paddling discipline. British Canoe Union (BCU) certification is also an excellent credential. Many states require summer-camp staff teaching canoeing or kayaking to be certified, although the levels of certification and specific requirements vary tremendously from state to state. Remember that no matter how good the equipment or conservative the trip plan, the people make the difference in the event of an accident.

~ *Do you have a packet of information about the program?* Evaluate this packet on its thoroughness. If you are sending your child on a multi-day trip, determine if the itinerary is clear, if there are provisions for mishaps and for contacting you in case of emergency. Is there a complete gear checklist?

~ *May I have some names of references to call?* A strong organization should jump at this chance to brag about their programs.

Then, of course, you'll be required to sign a release of liability and acceptance of risk form. This can be a scary piece of paper. Lines such as "I hereby release and hold harmless ABC, Inc., from any liability as a result of acts of its negligence that may occur on my child's trip," can scare parents away from any paddling program. Some parents see these forms as a clear indication that the organization asking them to sign such a release is trying to cover for its own incompetence.

In most cases the opposite is true. Any program seeking insurance through a reputable company will be required as a condition of that coverage to have all participants sign a waiver. The insurance company is trying to prevent paying for frivolous suits that may arise from participants claiming they did not understand the risks involved. The need to sign such an explicit release may appear to be a unique quirk of the paddling industry. A waiver, at the very least, can be a tool of communication between the paddling program, the child, and his parents.

CHAPTER EIGHT

KEEPING KIDS PADDLING SAFELY

There are kids who paddle and there are kids who are paddlers. Kids who paddle have been in a boat a few times and may even be adept at some of the physical skills, but they paddle only as long as it's convenient. Kids who are paddlers are into every aspect of the sport; it's often the center of their social lives, it's what they spend their birthday money on, and it's something they think about fanatically.

No matter how deeply paddling is ingrained in a kid's life, it can have a positive effect. Being a paddling fanatic is certainly not for everyone. We see some kids come and go in paddling; when the camp, school, or community program is over, they enjoyed their experiences, but go on to other pursuits and never look back. Others are interested in pursuing paddling, but lack the needed support structure. A few figure out how to pull together the necessary resources—a vehicle or a willing adult chauffeur, a boat and gear, and a knowledgeable group to go with—and take on paddling with a passion. Once kids have been introduced to paddling and show an interest in the sport, how do you ensure that they can pursue their interest?

~ PRACTICING AND ACQUIRING SKILLS ~

In order to keep paddling on their own, kids need solid skills above all else. As Becky Molina points out, "Skills are empowering for kids and they build confidence. Fun and love of the sport . . . follow naturally from that." Experiences in boats may give kids a taste of paddling, but to become real paddlers they need to go a step beyond. They need to develop a certain self-sufficiency. "Kids will continue to paddle because they know how to do something exciting with their boats, because they learned it in an instructional setting. A mere 'experience' can't always ensure that."

Ken Stone agrees: "I think that enjoyment of the sport is directly related to skill level. The students who have attained the greatest skills have the freedom to paddle the most difficult water and are often the ones who seem to stick with the sport. Few of my former students have continued to race, but many have continued to enjoy the recreational aspects of the sport. In addition, many have left the sport for a period of time and have picked it up again later in life when their circumstances were more amenable."

#8: Pack anything you don't want to get wet in a heavy-duty plastic bag inside a durable dry bag.

~ DEVELOPING JUDGMENT ~

When I was about sixteen my mother dropped me off at a roadside restaurant near our house obscenely early on a Saturday morning to catch a ride with another participant on a whitewater-canoeing weekend in the White Mountains of New Hampshire. As I hurriedly shuffled my gear from our family car to that of my ride for the weekend, my mother pulled me quickly aside as if to kiss me goodbye. I resisted the kiss, as any self-respecting sixteen-year-old would, but in the momentary void she slipped me a piece of advice I've never forgotten: "You know that you don't have to do anything you don't want to do on these trips, don't you?" she said. "Of course," I muttered back to her, but she completed her thought, "You have a good sense of self-preservation, so don't let any of the adults talk you into running rapids you don't want to run." "Yeah," I replied, and hustled over to the waiting car.

I thought about her advice a lot over the years, and now, with children of my own, I think about it in a different context. Judgment is not something kids get from reading a book, taking a class, or being told. They learn judgment through seeing it acted out by those around them whom they respect. Judgment comes into play anytime a long-term goal, such as personal survival, is put at risk by a short-term goal, such as ego gratification. When the rest of the group says they feel confident crossing a fog-shrouded open stretch of ocean, it takes a lot of gumption for the kid whose inner voice is expressing serious doubts to speak up. As a parent, I certainly hope my kids clearly express that they are not comfortable with such a decision.

What was so insightful about my mother's comment to me was that she understood that as a paddler in my own boat, making my own decisions, I would be in situations where I wanted to push my limits—run harder whitewater, paddle on a colder day—and ultimately those tough decisions of whether to proceed or not would be mine alone to make. She was expressing a confidence in my judgment and in turn reinforcing my own confidence in myself.

Kids often pick up skills so quickly that they are able to perform the athletic motions of paddling better than the adults around them in a short time. They can learn to launch themselves off waterfalls, surf the biggest waves, or paddle at the highest stroke rate with ease. Instilling in kids the judgment to decide when to turn back or not to go at all is much more difficult and involves more time than honing the physical skills to paddle.

The final word always lies with the adult leaders or the parents on a family trip, and the adults need to be comfortable with making tough decisions, even when they are unpopular ones. Turning back just short of a goal is never easy; it can cause tears and anger from kids who had been focusing on that goal, but it is far preferable to paddling after dark or spending an unprepared night outdoors.

Whether kids paddle with competent adults or more experienced kids, judgment should be approached as a topic of conversation and a valuable skill that each kid learns over a period of years. Only through supportive, open dialogue about judgment can kids learn to value their own intuitions and concerns, and make consistently solid decisions in the complex circumstances often encountered while paddling.

~ A PEER PADDLING NETWORK ~

While it is critical to teach kids a solid foundation of basic skills, kids are often the most motivated when they have the opportunity to improve their skills. Many kids thrive when they are put in an environment with other kids who are as good as or better than they.

Kids are their own best motivators.

Ken Stone has seen this happen with programs he has run and with kids he has coached on the United States Whitewater Team: "Peer groups determine the intensity of your program. If the group is highly competitive with each other, their skill level will most likely progress more quickly. If the group is less competitive, their skills are less likely to develop as keenly...."

In the Washington, D.C., area in the 1970s, Jon and Ron Lugbill, Bob Robison, David Hearn, and Kent Ford all discovered whitewater slalom racing at about the same time. They took up the solo closed canoe or C-1. They were teenagers and became close friends through their shared love of the sport. On weekends they would travel to races on the east coast together, and during the week they would paddle on the Potomac River that runs through the western suburbs and into downtown Washington, D.C. They would push each other to learn new skills, to design new boats, and eventually, to invent new techniques that now form the basis of modern whitewater techniques.

By 1975 Bob had qualified for the United States team and went to race in the World Championships in Europe. Over the next decade the five friends formed the core of the United States C-1 team and dominated the C-1 class worldwide. It's amazing what a few kids can accomplish just by playing around on a river.

CHAPTER NINE

TAKE A TRIP

Paddling far from civilization, camping with only what you've packed in your boat, and sleeping under a starry sky on a quiet beach with no sound except that of the waves splashing on the sand can create a lifetime of memories for both kids and their parents. Few experiences can be more energizing or sustain more lasting relationships than an extended wilderness or offshore paddling trip. Without the demands of daily life, kids and adults are free to explore at their leisure, talking, telling stories, or just enjoying quiet solitude—pleasures that our fast-paced world has made all too rare.

Taking kids on a first overnight paddling trip can feel like diving into a pool of murky water—you don't know for sure what you're going to encounter or how you and your kids will react to the experience. It helps to discuss the trip with your kids ahead of time and to give them as much of a role as possible in planning the route and packing the gear, so they are invested in the trip and have a sense of what it will be like.

It also helps to work into an extended paddling trip gradually. The chances of having a successful experience increase the more familiar kids already are with paddling. Introducing the sport to kids through a multi-day trip works well in many cases, but you risk finding that some kids aren't as taken with paddling as you'd hoped. Three days out with three days left to go is a tough time for you and them to discover this lack of interest.

Outfitters in the United States and worldwide offer two-day to multi-week, fully outfitted, "soft adventure" trips that are appropriate for kids and families. With an outfitter you minimize the burden of planning and ensure that one or several experienced guides can reduce the risks inherent in any outdoor, multi-day adventure. These fully outfitted trips are a great way to see some beautiful areas with minimal commitment. They are ideal for less-experienced paddlers who are not comfortable going out on their own or for those without the time or inclination to plan their own logistics. Many summer camps offer multi-day paddling trips and are terrific places for kids to be exposed to paddling in the wilderness for the first time.

PRIVATE PROPERTY AND PERMISSION

When paddling, it is best to consider all land private unless it is clearly posted as public land. Few landowners post their property along shorelines. Nonetheless, do not beach your boat on unposted or private property without getting permission first. Rivers are open to the public for paddling, but shorelines may be private; lakes may have a public boat ramp, but no public land to beach your boat. When you are paddling with tired kids who desperately need a break, you could find yourself with nowhere to stop.

Plan ahead! Take a map with you on your paddling trip and review it with your kids before setting out. Know in advance the location of public areas for rest stops. Your kids will be happy to know that a break is just around the bend.

How do you know if you have the experience needed to plan and lead your own extended paddling adventure? You should consider your skills in two general areas: *paddling* and *general outdoor skills*.

In the *paddling* arena, your skills should exceed those needed to deal with the worst conditions you could encounter. If you expect to paddle across a lake, consider whether you could handle your boat confidently if the wind picked up, the waves grew larger, and it started raining. To run a Class II whitewater river your own skills should allow you to handle Class III water readily. You don't want to simply survive in the conditions you'll encounter, you want to be able to handle them with little concern for your own needs. If you are not completely comfortable yourself, you won't be able to help the kids. When Alison and Kevin Sparks first started taking longer sea kayaking trips with their daughter, they brought along a third adult as a safety backup in case things got rough. This ensured that in the event of a mishap at least one adult would be able to focus on the child.

The *general outdoor skills* needed to plan and carry out your own multi-day paddling adventure vary from area to area and from season to season. Camping skills, map-reading ability, first-aid knowledge, and basic knowledge of weather and tides are all essential for a successful trip.

~ Planning for Extended Trips ~

Parents often spend weeks or months planning for a trip in the hope of remembering to pack every last piece of gear they'll need and to plan for every possible emergency. When you get on the water, as long as you have the basic equipment you need for a safe trip, forgetting to bring a treasured toy or a favorite snack is not a big deal.

The site you choose for your first extended trip will depend greatly on your paddling experience, the time and money you have available, and your risk tolerance. A small lake with campsites around it offers a perfect low-risk location for a first multi-day paddle. Look for a place where the distances between campsites can be covered in a couple of hours or less. Many lakes have trails around their perimeters that link the campsites, allowing a retreat by foot if needed. A calm river with closely-spaced campsites also works well. Canoe rental services are available on many rivers, providing the boat and paddles, and often transporting you before or after the trip, renting you camping gear, and helping you plan your route.

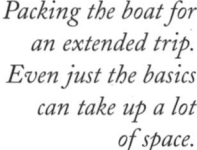
Packing the boat for an extended trip. Even just the basics can take up a lot of space.

Alison Sparks warns that it is important to have several alternative float plans in mind, especially when planning a trip offshore where conditions can vary from windless and calm to stormy with large, breaking waves. The four alternatives to consider are: what you would like to do; a sized-down version of what you would like to do; what you would do in very protected waters; and a fun land-based alternative you can do, while postponing the paddling trip to a later date with safer conditions.

With kids younger than fourteen, plan to paddle no more than half the distance you would paddle with an all-adult group each day. It is reasonable to expect to cover fifteen miles or so in a day on the ocean with competent adults and favorable conditions. With young kids along, seven miles may be more realistic. Even if you've set up the boats so only the adults paddle and the kids go along for the ride, Alison Sparks limits stretches of uninterrupted paddling to no more than an hour. "Break up the trip with games, landings, water play, etc...There's nothing worse than a screaming kid throwing a tantrum on a crossing, with cold ocean spray whipping away the last of your psychological reserve." It is always better to have kid send the day wishing they could paddle more than the other way around.

LEAVE NO TRACE

Here are some important principles, in kid friendly terms, to remember and practice while you are enjoying the outdoors, courtesy of Leave No Trace—a national educational program that promotes skills and ethics to support the sustainable use of natural areas.

Know before you go. *Be prepared! The more you know, the more fun you will have.*

Choose the right path. *Use existing camp areas and walk on the main trail to protect nature.*

Trash your trash. *Pack it in, pack it out. Put litter in trash cans or carry it home. Keep water clean. Don't put soap or food in lakes or streams.*

Leave what you find. *Leave plants, rocks, and historical items as you find them so the next person can enjoy them.*

Be careful with fire. *Use a gas-fueled camp stove for cooking. It's easier to cook on and clean up than a fire. If it's OK to build a campfire in the area you're visiting, use an existing fire ring to protect the ground from heat.*

Respect wildlife. *Watch wildlife from a distance and never approach, feed, or follow them.*

Be kind to other visitors. *Make sure the fun you have in the outdoors does not bother anyone else. Remember that other visitors are there to enjoy nature.*

Teach your kids Leave No Trace principles and practice what you preach; they will learn to respect nature and become stewards of the outdoor places they love. For more information on Leave No Trace see page 168.

#9: Protect children from the sun—routinely apply plenty of waterproof sunscreen (with SPF 30 or more) and a broad-brimmed hat that won't blow off in the wind.

MY ISLAND GIRL

BY ALISON SPARKS

It all started during a clean-up on Strawberry Island. Kevin and Lena circled to the right and I circled to the left. When we met on the far rocks with our trash bags, my husband Kevin and I had independently revamped our upcoming camping vacation: scrap the trip to the pond and break Lena in on a Maine island. Lena, our 2-year-old veteran camper and kayaker, had never kayak camped and the upcoming Fourth of July weekend had been targeted for a three-night adventure on a northern Vermont pond. But the island magic of a sparkling day in early June transformed our plans to a favorite destination—somewhere on the Maine Island Trail.

So began several weeks of furious activity. Nights were spent poring over the guidebook and charts. Equipment lists were revised, safety gear redesigned. We picked the brains of Maine Island Trail Association members for local island knowledge, trying to choose the perfect island, taking into consideration the whims of kids and weather risks. We mentally measured up our paddling friends to figure out who would enjoy paddling at a kid's pace and left tempting invitations on Jim and Lola's answering machines.

The double kayak was hauled in and out of the basement weekly for trial packs and practice sessions on the local pond. Unfortunately, Lena liked swimming in her PFD so much, she preferred jumping out of the boat rather than climbing in. The temperature of the ocean water reversed that cycle.

We investigated the possibility of stuffing a toddler into a wetsuit and bought a toddler-sized version on the spot at a local outdoor store. The salesman wryly commented, "For the kid who has everything...." One alteration session fit the wetsuit reasonably well to Lena's rotund figure.

Trip plans began to coalesce. Lola left a return message, "Found dogsitter. Psyched. Where're we going?" Jim was also game from the start. A week before the trip, we began listening to the weather radio twice a day. A bad forecast would keep us close to home (Muscongus Bay). A good forecast meant Penobscot Bay or bust. One last midnight sewing session finished a tow rope assembly. We were red-eyed but ready. On the early side of the holiday weekend, Lena, Kevin, and I headed to Augusta where we met Jim and Lola. The next morning, under clear blue skies, all five of us ate our last mainland meal and caravanned to Naskeag Point. On the cobblestone beach, we paddlers labored at boat-packing while Lena collected ballast. When everyone was ready to go, Lena climbed into the open middle hatch of our double kayak, where two large jugs of water were stored with the spouts tucked out of reach of a toddler. (Water conservation lessons started at the launch site when Lena was caught blithely watering her middle hatch.)

After landing just north of Naskeag Harbor, we hopped over to Hog Island, took a cookie break on Little Hog, followed the shore to Devil's Head, and nosed the kayak to a bearing for Sellers Island, which had by now become shrouded by fog. For the first time, the sound of waves breaking in the *fog stirred up motherly doubts—what were we doing with a kid in an open hatch on the ocean heading into the grayness? Five minutes later, as we landed on the pink beach of Sellers, a sunbeam parted the fog.*

Our island was magnificent. The green-blue water curled onto an expanse of beach that dared the granite to encroach. Lena was thrilled. She tumbled up the beach, slipped up and down the rocks, and managed the tree-root staircase with a boost from behind. After supervising our camp setup, she promptly requested a nap and burrowed into her pile blankets. A few minutes later Jim emerged from the pine grove and reported, "I don't understand everything Lena's saying, but I distinctly heard 'kayak' and 'away in Maine'." Lena quickly adjusted to an island pace. The days were simple, dozing in the sun, combing through periwinkle beds, and chasing miniature crustaceans across the tide pools.

Glassy seas and a promise of light winds heralded our second morning, furnishing perfect conditions for a paddle to Potato Island. As the boats glided southward, Lena's usual chatter dwindled to nothing. She had never seen such an expanse of water—where was that comforting shoreline? The diversion of looking for lobster buoys quickly raised her spirits. Potato offered warm, granite tide pools where we played for several hours.

On the final morning of our trip, we reluctantly packed the boats on a falling tide. The pink beach glistened and beckoned. Lena stalled. Only with the promise of another kayak camping trip did she climb back into her hatch. We dipped our paddles in farewell as my island girl settled in for a nap.

CHAPTER TEN

COMPETITIVE PADDLING OPPORTUNITIES FOR KIDS

Nothing beats competitive paddling as a way to raise any paddler's skills, hone their appreciation for the sport, and give them opportunities to test themselves against their peers. The opportunities to compete are plentiful and the community of competitors in all paddling disciplines is small, tight-knit, and generally very supportive of newcomers. Most of these disciplines have a national governing body that makes rules, sanctions competitions, and promotes the sport. These are listed in Appendix C.

~ FREESTYLE CANOEING ~

Freestyle canoeing is the closest equivalent paddling has to ballet. In freestyle the paddler or paddlers come up with choreographed routines that often are performed to music. Freestyle invites innovation and expressiveness. Kids are naturals at freestyle. As Becky Molina points out, with its small participant base, "the freestyle community is a wonderful family that cherishes its children, making them feel like the proverbial million bucks. Not many kids can take paddlesport instruction [from,] then have lunch with, the national champions in their sport."

~ MARATHON CANOE RACING ~

Marathon canoeing is similar to its twenty-six-mile terra-firma counterpart with races of ten miles or more. The canoes are streamlined; they are built for straight-line speed and do not turn easily. The paddlers train to build aerobic endurance so they can maintain high stroke rates over long distances. A teen who likes to canoe and shows an interest in the competitive side of the sport may do well in marathon canoeing.

~ FLATWATER RACING (SPRINT) ~

Flatwater racing has been an Olympic sport since 1924, and is a cousin to marathon canoeing. The boats are built for nothing but speed on flatwater, so they turn only with lots of persuasion and are very tippy and narrow.

~ WHITEWATER SLALOM ~

Slalom paddling consists of maneuvering in and out of twenty to twenty-five gates hung across a section of whitewater. The challenge is to control the boat on the whitewater while maintaining precise moves through the gates without hitting them. At the elite level, this sport takes considerable training and comfort running whitewater. When gates are used on flatwater or easy whitewater, kids who are already paddling whitewater boats can benefit from learning to move through the gates. Running gates on easy water develops stroke timing, precision, and boat control. Kids can have fun doing mock races down the course. Some secondary schools have slalom teams that train on nearby rivers and attend races in spring and fall.

Slalom racing is a great way for kids to learn to compete in a positive way outdoors. Photo courtesy of Adventure Quest.

~ Downriver Racing ~

Downriver boats are like their flatwater-sprint cousins; they're designed to go fast in a straight line. On whitewater, however, these boats need to maneuver around rocks and obstacles, so they are designed to turn better than flatwater boats. Downriver boats are long, with lots of volume, and are rather tippy at first. Kids can have fun using downriver boats on flatwater to improve their balance.

~ Whitewater Rodeo ~

This is the newest form of paddling and probably one of the fastest-growing areas of the sport. In rodeo paddling, the boats are ultra-short (eight feet and under) and the maneuvers are acrobatic, resembling those of a skateboarder. One of the nicest things about rodeo is that you don't need a long stretch of rapids to have a blast. "Park and play" boating, where boaters drive to a rapid and work with a single feature for hours on end, is becoming the norm in some parts of the country. Since rodeo is all about playing, kids excel at it. Kids as young as ten can learn to "throw ends" or cartwheel, one of the basic rodeo moves. Several new boat designs are geared toward kids and small adults, making rodeo a great choice for kids who are competent whitewater boaters and want to take the sport to another level.

Rodeo helps kids learn to focus in chaotic surroundings while having a blast. Photo courtesy of Adventure Quest.

We received a Christmas letter from friends, Klaus and Tanya, putting it all into perspective: "We competed in all nine of the New England Slalom Series whitewater races this year, something we've never attempted before. The boys competed in C-2 (two-person covered canoe) with me. The competition was often quite close between the team of Ansel/Klaus and the team of Tollan/Klaus. We also were quite successful against other teams, placing in almost every race. I am amazed at how strong both Tollan and Ansel have gotten at canoeing. They can really move the bow around, as well as provide surprising forward power. We bought kayaks for the boys and spent many afternoons on local lakes and slow, meandering rivers. Learning to paddle a solo kayak is a bit more complicated than the bow position in the C-2, but progress is steady and usually fun. The boys are starting to try easy rapids now."

Safety Tip

#10: Insect repellent is often necessary when paddling. Repellent should contain less than 10 percent DEET for children under twelve, and children should never apply repellent themselves.

AFTERWORD

CANOEING ON THE GREEN RIVER

BY BRUCE LESSELS

As we bumped and clattered down the washboard road leading to Mineral Bottom, Abbie made her way to the front seat to sit next to me. I yelled above the sound of the bus, "That must be the river canyon over there." I pointed to a distant depression in the otherwise flat, brown land-scape. The bus driver called back to me, "That's just a wash. The Green River is still a ways ahead of us."

Our teeth chattered from the vibrations. Abbie shifted over to sit next to mom. The kids behind me absentmind-edly looked out the windows. The difficulty of being heard kept conversation to short exchanges. Soon we slowed, as the sharp edge of a canyon appeared ahead of us. The land dropped suddenly away a thousand feet below us. The bus driver turned off the engine and announced we would take a photo and bathroom break before descending to the floor of the canyon. We filed out of the bus. Women and girls went to the left, men and boys to the right.

Tyler came over and peered over the edge with me. I warned him not to get too close. He moved a half step back and kept looking over the edge. I asked him how his broken arm was feeling. "Fine," he said curtly and ran back to the bus.

When the bus was reloaded and the driver had checked to be sure there were no other vehicles coming up the road, we started down the first steep switchback in lowest gear.

The bus whined and the driver patiently steered his way along the one-lane dirt track. "I don't drive this road when it rains," he said when we first started onto the flat, bumpy part several miles back. I could see why. If you put a tire off the edge here, you'd come to rest a thousand feet below, flat as a pancake. I admired his patience as I took in the view of the canyon.

At the bottom, an oasis of green appeared almost artificial in the midst of the desert scenery. The river was visible here and there where the vegetation was not so dense, but the pale green of the leaves dominated the river itself. The color changed abruptly as I looked up the far side of the Green River canyon and scanned the endless cliffs of red, gray, white, and green sandstone and limestone, exposed by the action of the river over millions of years.

On a sharp switchback about two-thirds of the way down, we met another truck that pulled over to let us pass. As we slowly rounded the corner, we looked over the edge of the road and saw a flattened car in several indistinguishable pieces, like scree scattered on the edge of the cliff. An image of the car rolling down the mountain came into my head, and I focused on our destination just beyond the green area at the bottom of the canyon to erase the car from my mind.

When no more sharp turns were between us and the flat bottom of the road, the driver shifted into a higher gear and the bus went from a crawl to about thirty miles per hour, as we traversed the last mile to Mineral Bottom and the beginning of our five-day adventure on the Green River.

With four adults and five children, we had originally planned on taking four canoes, but seven-year-old Tyler had broken his arm and would not be able to help his mom paddle. We agreed that if we could fit all our gear and kids into three boats, we would gain a paddling advantage by *having one boat paddled by two adults. We settled on bringing four boats to the put-in, but trying to fit everything into three. If it worked, we would send a boat back with the bus.*

The pile of gear on the ground behind the truck appeared massive. While the five kids ate lunch, played together, and burned off the nervous energy they had built up in anticipation of the trip, the four adults worked on distributing and packing gear in the boats. My boat was loaded with two large drybags, a box full of pots and pans, a five-gallon jug of water, and a few odds and ends—that was just in the middle. Behind my stern seat I fit another drybag and some spare river shoes. In front another bag of water fit easily under the bow deck plate.

When we finished organizing and cramming gear wherever we could, the three boats were stuffed, but all the gear had fit. Now for the kids. Their primary concern was who got to go in Darcy's boat. At 10 years old, she was the big kid and the spot in front of her bow seat was coveted by the others. Sitting in front of Darcy came to mean you would be treated to wonderful stories about the exploits of Klebob the bear and Freddy the pelican as we paddled past endless walls of red and white sandstone.

The first day we traveled ten miles in a couple of hours, putting to rest any doubts I had about bringing so much gear in just three boats. In the bow of my boat, seven-year-old Abbie paddled a little. Her four-year-old sister, Hannah, sat on the pile of gear in the middle and took a few strokes herself. Mostly the sisters just watched the cliffs go by, talking about the shapes they imagined in the rocks, and trying to egg me on to race the other boats.

By 4:30 P.M. we were at the first campsite and unloading gear. The kids played on the upstream end of the beach while the adults set up tents and began cooking on the downstream end. After a spaghetti dinner and a short time telling stories by the campfire, everybody crawled into sleeping bags and quickly fell off to sleep. The next morning we went for a hike, and by noon we were packed up and back on the river.

The kids were doing great and between singing, telling stories and jokes, and occasionally paddling, they seemed to be enjoying the trip. I explained several times to Hannah that she should sit in the middle of the boat; she didn't really understand why until my paddle unexpectedly hit a snag underwater and I leaned abruptly overboard to retrieve it. After that, she needed only an occasional reminder.

Late in the afternoon we came to the only rapidlike stretch on the trip—a hundred-yard-long section of fast, choppy water. By this time, Karen was paddling in the bow and Abbie sat on the floor of the boat in front of her. Karen and I decided to turn into the eddy at the base of the rapid. As the boat swung quickly around, Abbie protested. We assured her that the chances of flipping were slim, but she didn't buy it and we passed up a few tempting eddies downstream.

Our second campsite was also on a sandy beach, but here the canyon was narrower and felt more confining.

On the third morning, we all began stirring just before sunrise. Jamie was up first and had the hot water on the stove. Shortly after, a couple of kids rose, and by 7:30 A.M. our campsite was bustling with kids eating, brushing teeth, changing into warm clothes (and then an hour or so later, back into shorts and T-shirts as the sun rose over the canyon walls). We broke camp in under an hour—a pretty quick take-down considering the amount of gear we had and the number of kids we were mobilizing—and we were on the river before 10 A.M.

As we paddled and floated downstream, we debated whether we should do a long (twenty-mile) day and then lay over a day at the next campsite, or whether it would be too much for the kids. By lunchtime we had covered ten miles and the kids were in good spirits; we decided to push on. By 3:30 P.M. we were all starting to lose steam, and Abbie in my bow, and Tyler in the middle, both declared they had to go to the bathroom and couldn't wait the twenty minutes or so until we pulled in at the final campsite.

After finding an appropriate place to "use the bathroom," Abbie whined that she was too tired to continue. "Hop in the boat and we'll be there in no time," I said.

Tyler joined in the chorus, "I'm not getting in the boat. I'm too tired," he said.

"We can't camp here," I replied and tried to coax them back into the boat with descriptions of dinner and the wonderful fun things to do just a short distance downstream. My own patience was wearing thin.

"How about if we try fishing for the last little bit?" I asked. That piqued their interest and Tyler came back into the boat.

I pulled out the collapsible fishing pole and tied a lure on the line, which we dangled in the current behind the boat. Abbie held the tip of the rod out away from the boat so the line wouldn't tangle with my paddle. In a few minutes she tired of holding the rod; Tyler held it briefly but also lost interest. I took it from him, held it with my knee against the gunwale for a few minutes, and then reeled in the line as we rounded the last bend of the day. A quarter-mile ahead on the right bank, two canoes sat at the mouth of Jasper Canyon. Our long day was at an end, and the kids were still hanging in there. We passed the last minutes before tying up to shore discussing dinner options and who was going to sleep out under the stars that night.

On the final day, Abbie and Tyler were again in my
boat, but they decided to sit two abreast on the bow seat.
They both had pads of paper and were writing and drawing as we passed through the end of Labyrinth Canyon and
approached the confluence with the Colorado River, where
we were to be picked up by a jet boat. The hour-long paddle
was pleasant in the slightly cooler weather that had come in
the night before.

In a broad left turn the cliffs leaned away from us and
the walls above the Colorado indicated the end of our journey. Abbie and Tyler were laughing, talking, drawing, and
making jokes that only seven-year-olds truly appreciate. I
told them the Colorado was ahead; they ignored me and
kept on playing. When we landed at the beach where we
were to be picked up, the five kids immediately banded
together and started playing a game; Tyler was pretending
to shoot the rest of us for no apparent reason. Jamie and I
joined in briefly; though I was shot quickly. We made lunch
and tried to interest the kids in eating. They ate in between
rounds of the game as we waited for the jet boat, and I mar-
velled at what good friends they had become in our five
days on the river.

*Sharing stories
around the camp-
fire after a day on
the Green River.*

APPENDIX A

GLOSSARY OF TERMS

Bow: The front of a boat.

Bow draw: A duffek stroke that is pulled toward the bow of the boat for additional turning effect.

Brace: A stroke performed with the paddle blade flat on the surface of the water to support some or all of the paddler's weight and prevent capsizing.

Closed canoe: A specialized whitewater canoe with a small cockpit similar to a kayak. In a closed canoe, however, the paddler kneels and uses a single-bladed paddle.

Cockpit: The opening in the deck of a kayak where the paddler sits.

Cross draw: A stroke only done in a solo canoe or the bow of a tandem canoe that pulls the bow of the boat toward the side opposite the side on which the canoeist normally holds her paddle. Performed by crossing the paddle over the boat without changing the grip on the paddle and pulling the boat toward the paddle.

Current differential: An area where two currents meet.

Draw stroke: A stroke in a canoe or a kayak that pulls the boat toward the paddle.

Dry Bag: A nearly waterproof rubberized bag with either a roll-down or a zip-type closure. They are available in a range of sizes.

Duffek stroke: Also known as a stationary draw or a bow rudder. This static stroke is held in front of the paddler and at an angle to the boat and guides the boat toward the paddle by taking advantage of existing boat speed or current speed.

Eddy: An area of calm water behind a rock or other obstruction in a river. Eddies are often used by whitewater paddlers as stopping places in the middle of rapids.

Eddy line: An area of whirlpools and turbulence caused by upstream-moving eddy water moving past downstream-moving current.

Eddy turn: A maneuver used to enter an eddy. The paddler drives his boat toward the eddy line at about a forty-five-degree angle. As the boat crosses the eddy line the paddler leans into the eddy and places a stationary draw stroke to act as a pivot on the inside of the turn.

Eskimo roll: A technique for righting an upside-down kayak or canoe without exiting the cockpit.

Ferry: A maneuver that allows a paddler to cross from one side of a moving river to the other without moving downstream.

Forward stroke: A stroke taken to propel a canoe, kayak, or raft in a forward direction.

Grab loop: A short loop of rope or handle placed near each end of a canoe or kayak designed for rescues or as a means to carry the boat.

Gunwale: The rail around the outside of a canoe that acts as a stiffener, helping the boat maintain its shape.

Hands roll: An Eskimo roll done without using a paddle.

Otter entry: A spectacular-looking method of entering the water by sliding off a cliff or bank adjacent to the water.

Peel out: A maneuver in which a paddler leaves an eddy by paddling into the current, leaning downstream and allowing the current to turn the boat downstream.

Planing hull: A type of hull design made popular in whitewater rodeo kayaks where the bottom of the boat is very flat and the sides form nearly right angles to the bottom. Boats with planing hulls sit on top of the water when surfing a wave, enabling them to do tricks such as spins that require the boat to break free of the surface of the water.

Rocker: The amount of front-to-back curvature in the hull of the boat.

Skeg: A two- to six-inch long protrusion from the bottom of the stern of a kayak that helps the boat stay on a straight course.

Sprayskirt: A piece of equipment designed to seal a kayak or canoe's cockpit opening to prevent water from getting in.

Stern: The back of a boat.

Surf: To ride a wave or other river or ocean feature in a similar manner to board surfers.

Sweep stroke: A stroke in a canoe or kayak in which the paddler uses the paddle blade to describe a wide arc around himself from bow to stern, causing the boat to move forward and turn away from the paddle side. In a reverse sweep the paddler describes a similar arc but starts the paddle at the stern and moves it toward the bow causing the boat to move backward and turn toward the paddle side.

Track: To go in a straight line. A boat with a pronounced keel and little rocker will track better than one with a flat hull and considerable rocker.

Wave train: A series of standing waves in which the first wave is usually the largest, the second is usually the steepest, and the rest get smaller moving downstream.

Wet exit: To exit the cockpit of a canoe or kayak from underwater.

Yaw: The side-to-side motion a kayak often makes due to the alteration of strokes on one side and then the other.

APPENDIX B

GENERAL CHARACTERISTICS OF KAYAKS AND CANOES

Kayaks and canoes come in a variety of shapes and sizes. Selecting the right boat for your needs will enhance your fun, safety, and comfort.

Design	Intended Uses	Length Range	Materials
Recreational	lakes, easy rivers	9'–14'	plastic
Touring	treks of one day, or a week or more	12'–19'	plastic composite
Sit-on-top	lakes, rivers, ocean surf	9'–14'	plastic
Whitewater	whitewater rivers, ocean surf	7'–12'	plastic composite

General Characteristics of Kayaks

pprox. Weight Range	Approx. Price Range	Comments
30–80 lbs	$300–$800	For fooling around in at the lake, paddling out to an island, or fishing. Very stable and wide, and available in one- and two-person models.
50–100 lbs	$800–$1500	Heavy but very durable.
30–60 lbs	$1400–$3000	Significantly lighter than plastic boats and come in a wider variety of designs. Serious sea kayakers use composite boats.
40–90 lbs	$300–$800	Good for kids who are not comfortable wet exiting from a sit-inside boat. Seat is molded right into the deck.
30–50 lbs	$700–$1100	Very durable.
20–40 lbs	$1200–$1800	Lightweight and easy for kids to move, but very expensive.

General Characteristics of Canoes

Design	Intended Uses	Length Range	Materials
General purpose recreation	lakes, easy rivers, mild whitewater	15'–17'	Royalex/plastic
			fiberglass/composite
			wood
			aluminum
Whitewater tandem	Class II and above whitewater	15'–16'	Royalex
			composite
Whitewater solo	Class II and above whitewater	10'–15'	Royalex
			composite
Tripping	multi-day outings with gear; flatwater to Class III whitewater	16'–18'	Royalex
			composite
Marathon racing	fast downriver or flatwater sprints	15'–18'	composite

Approx. Weight Range	Approx. Price Range	Comments
70–90 lbs	$400–$1300	Great for families.
50–90 lbs	$300–$2000	Low-end fiberglass boats can be inexpensive, but are heavy and not very durable. Expensive composite boats are very light and tough.
60–80 lbs	$1000–$2500	Not durable and might require maintenance.
70–90 lbs	$500–$800	Tough, heavy, and noisy.
70–90 lbs	$700–$1200	Royalex boats are the toughest for whitewater but are heavier than composites.
50–80 lbs	$1000–$1500	Lighter and available in more designs than Royalex, but require patching.
45–65 lbs	$600–$1100	See above.
30–50 lbs	$900–$1400	See above.
70–90 lbs	$800–$1300	Durable but heavy to portage.
50–80 lbs	$1200–$3000	Lighter weight can make a difference on portages, but is it worth the cost?
30–60 lbs	$1200–$3000	Tippy, very fast, and fun. Small kids can make these go fast.

PADDLING PROGRAMS

Camps

For a full listing of camps that offer canoeing and kayaking programs visit the American Camping Association's website at www.acacamps.org.

Appalachian Mountain Club
Teen Wilderness Adventures
(in conjunction with Great Glen Trails Outdoor Center)
P.O. Box 298
Gorham, NH 03581-0298
603-466-2727
www.outdoors.org

Camp Mondamin
P.O. Box 8
Tuxedo, NC 28784
800-688-5789
www.mondamin.com

Camp Chewonki
485 Chewonki Neck Road
Wiscasset, ME 04578
207-882-7323
www.chewonki.org

Valley Mill Camp
15101 Seneca Road
Darnestown, MD 20874
301-948-0220
www.valleymill.com

Kroka Expeditions
659 West Hill Road
Putney, VT 05346
802-387-5397
www.kroka.com

Challenge Wilderness Camps
Country Grove 4
300 North Grove Street
Rutland, VT 05701
800-832-4295
www.challengewilderness.com

Schools

Salisbury School
251 Canaan Road
Salisbury, CT 06068
860-435-5700
www.salisburyschool.org

Proctor Academy
P.O. Box 500
Andover, NH 03216
603-735-6212
www.proctoracademy.org

Academy at Charlemont
Mohawk Trail
Charlemont, MA 01339
413-339-4912
www.charlemont.org

Outfitters

Cascade Kayak School
7050 Highway 55
Horseshoe Bend, ID 83629
800-292-7238
www.cascaderaft.com

Current Adventures
P.O. Box 828
Lotus, CA 95651
888-4KAYAKING
www.adventuresports.com/kayak/current/welcome.htm

Endless River Adventures
14157 Highway 19 West
P.O. Box 246
Bryson City, NC 28713
828-488-6199
www.endlessriveradventures.com

Four Corners Paddling School
P.O. Box 379
Durango, CO 81302
800-426-7637
www.paddleschool.com

Zoar Outdoor
P.O. Box 245
Charlemont, MA 01339
800-532-7483
www.zoaroutdoor.com

Nantahala Outdoor Center
13077 Highway 19 West
Bryson City, NC 28713
800-232-7238
www.noc.com

Riversport School of Kayaking
P.O. Box 95
Confluence, PA 15424
800-216-6991
www.shol.com/kayak/index.htm

Cape Cod Kayak
P.O. Box 1273
North Falmouth, MA 02556
508-540-9377
www.capecodkayak.com

PADDLING EQUIPMENT FOR KIDS

Companies that currently make child-sized gear are listed here. Since the youth market is growing constantly, look for more companies to be producing kid-sized gear in the future. Most paddling magazines produce annual buyer's guides that are good sources of up-to-date information on kids' gear.

PFDs

~ Extrasport has a full line of child and youth vests— 800-633-0837, www.extrasport.com.

~ Lotus Designs has a vest for kids weighing 50–90 pounds— 828-689-2470, www.lotusdesigns.com.

~ Stearns makes infant, child, and youth vests for all types of watersports—800-697-5801, www.stearnsinc.com.

~ MTI Adventure Wear makes vests for kids weighing 30–50 and 50–90 pounds—800-783-4684, www.mtiadventurewear.com.

~ Old Town Canoe Company has vests for kids weighing 50–70 and 70–90 pounds—800-595-4400, www.otccanoe.com.

Listed below are manufacturers that make boats specifically for kids; however, lots of boats that are designed for small adults are also suitable for larger kids.

Canoes

~ Mohawk Canoes has smaller solo recreational canoes for kids that can be paddled tandem—800-686-6429, www.mohawkcanoes.com.

~ Old Town Canoe Company has two canoes suitable for kids to paddle tandem or solo—800-595-4400, www.otccanoe.com.

~ Wenonah Canoe has smaller recreational canoes for kids to paddle tandem—507-454-5430, www.wenonah.com.

Touring Boats

~ Chesapeake Light Craft makes a fourteen-foot touring kayak for kids 60–130 pounds—410-267-0137, www.clcboats.com.

~ Hydra Kayaks has a kid's touring kayak—800-537-8888, www.rotocast.com/hydra.

~ Old Town Canoe Company has a kid's recreational kayak—800-595-4400, www.otccanoe.com.

~ Perception has a recreational kayak for kids—800-59-KAYAK, www.kayaker.com.

~ Pygmy Boats, Inc., has a few recreational kayaks for kids weighing 30–60 and 70–140 pounds—360-385-6143, www.pygmyboats.com.

~ Wilderness Systems has a kid's touring boat—800-311-7245, www.wildernesssytems.com.

Whitewater Boats

~ Dagger has several whitewater kayaks for kids 65–135 and 85–150 pounds—423-882-0404, www.dagger.com.

~ Necky has several smaller boats that kids can use—
604-850-1206, www.necky.com.

~ Perception has a whitewater kayak for kids weighing 50–135
pounds—800-59-KAYAK, www.kayaker.com.

~ Pyranha/Impex has a whitewater kayak for kids weighing
70–110 pounds—828-299-1523, www.impexkayak.com.

~ Riot Kayaks has one design for kids weighing 80–130
pounds—514-931-0366, www.riotkayaks.com.

~ The Upstream Edge makes composite whitewater kayaks with
several designs for kids—519-824-1415,
www.rockwood-outfitters.com.

~ Wavesport has a whitewater kayak for kids weighing 65–110
pounds—800-311-7245, www.wavesport.com.

Sit-on-Top Kayaks (SOT)

~ Cobra Kayaks has an SOT that is small enough to be used
solo or tandem by kids—310-327-9216,
www.cobrakayaks.com.

~ Ocean Kayak has an SOT specifically designed for kids up to
150 pounds—800-8-KAYAKS, www.oceankayak.com.

~ Trinity Bay Kayaks has an SOT for smaller adults and kids—
800-311-7245, www.trinitybaykayaks.com.

Inflatables

~ Custom Inflatables has designed two inflatable kayaks for
kids—800-6-SEEKER, www.tseeker.com.

~ Stearns Inc. has an inflatable youth kayak—320-252-1642,
www.stearnsinc.com.

~ Innova produces a kid's inflatable kayak for flatwater—
425-776-1171, www.innovakayak.com.

Paddles

~ Werner Paddles has smaller touring paddles for kids—800-275-3311, www.wernerpaddles.com.

~ Mitchell Paddles has whitewater paddles for kids—603-523-7004, www.mitchellpaddles.com.

~ Ainsworth Paddles has whitewater paddles for kids—800-688-3792, www.ainsworthpaddles.com.

~ Harmony has touring paddles for kids—864-859-7518, www.harmonygear.com.

~ Wildwasser had several whitewater paddles for kids—303-444-2336, www.wildnet.com.

~ Old Town Canoe Company has a number of canoe and kayak paddles sized for kids—207-827-5513, www.otccanoe.com.

Other Gear

~ Kokatat makes kid-sized jackets, drysuits, and pants—800-225-9749, www.kokatat.com.

~ Northwest River Supply has kids' wetsuits—800-635-5202, www.nrsweb.com.

~ Teva makes kids' sandals and other outdoor footwear—800-367-8382, www.teva.com.

~ Voyageur has paddling gear—800-311-7245, www.voyageur-gear.com.

~ Harmony has paddling accessories—864-859-7518, www.harmonygear.com.

APPENDIX E

PADDLING RESOURCES

Websites

Many websites have club listings, gear information, e-mail newsletters, trip itineraries, tide information, and river-gauge levels.

ACAnet.org: recreational paddling, conservation policies and efforts, events and instruction, and online shop.

adventuresports.com/paddlesports: gear, outfitters, clubs, and general paddling resources.

Americanwhitewater.org: national river policy and conservation member organization, listings of rodeo races.

americaoutdoors.org: outfitter and guide services database directory by state and extensive trip planning.

amrivers.org: conservation and policy news, trips, and a kid's page.

GORP.com/activity/paddling: paddling section for whitewater, kayak touring, and rafting, news, gear, trips, and discussion.

Outdoors.org: Appalachian Mountain Club website, a resource on conservation, recreation, and education in the Northeast.

Outdoorplay.com: online paddling gear store, club listing by state, and events.

Riversport.com: extensive paddling club listing.

usacanoekayak.org: national governing body of Olympic paddling.

Magazines

Atlantic Coastal Kayaker: P.O. Box 520, Ipswich, MA 01938.

Canoe and Kayak Magazine: P.O. Box 3146, Kirkland, WA 98083, 206-827-6363.

Che-Mun, The Journal of Canadian Wilderness Canoeing: Box 548, Station 0, Toronto, Ontario, Canada M4A2P1, 416-789-2142.

Confluence: 1343 North Portage, Palatine, IL 60067.

Folding Kayaker: P.O. Box 0754, New York, NY 10024, 212-724-5069.

Paddle Sport Magazine: Box 1388, Soquel, CA 95073.

Paddler Magazine: P.O. Box 1341, Eagle, ID 83616, 208-939-4500.

Sea Kayak Magazine: P.O. Box 17170, Seattle, WA 98107-0970, 206-789-9536.

Videos

No specific paddling videos are available for kids; however, some great paddling videos are out there that kids are sure to enjoy. Videos generally are distributed through dealers or large book stores like Barnes & Noble, Amazon.com, and Borders Books and Music. Performance Video also has a full line of paddling instruction videos, www.performancevideo.com.

Several good videos to start with include:

The Kayaker's Edge: basic to advanced whitewater techniques.

Whitewater Self Defense: rescue and safety techniques used on the water.

Performance Sea Kayaking: basic skills and paddling techniques for sea kayakers.

C-1 Challenge: instructional techniques for decked canoeists.

Solo Playboating: open canoe instruction for whitewater techniques.

The staff at Nantahala Outdoor Center has produced several instructional paddling videos:

Grace under Pressure: demonstrates the basics of an Eskimo roll.

Kayak 101: Mastering the Basics: basic skills for whitewater kayaking.

Other good videos include:

From Here to There: Canoe Basics: instructional techniques for novice to intermediate canoeists.

Kayaking Basics: featuring Olympic Gold Medalist Greg Barton, demonstrating flatwater kayak techniques for the ocean or easy rivers.

Surf Kayaking Fundamentals: surf zone and sea kayaking techniques.

Path of the Paddle: Quiet Water: Bill Mason's solo and tandem canoeing on flatwater.

Path of the Paddle: Whitewater: Bill Mason's solo and tandem canoeing on whitewater.

Classic Solo Canoeing: Becky Mason and Paul Wing, www.kineticvideo.com.

Books

Canoeing

Glaros, Lou and Charlie Wilson. *Freestyle Canoeing.* Birmingham, AL: Menasha Ridge Press, 1993.

Grant, Gordon. *Trailside Guide: Canoeing.* Scranton, PA: W. W. Norton and Company Inc., 1997.

Gullion, Laurie. *Canoeing (Outdoor Pursuits Series).* Champaign, IL: Human Kinetics Publishers, 1993.

Kuhne, Cecil. *Paddling Basics: Canoeing.* Mechanicsburg, PA: Stackpole Books, 1998.

Mason, Bill. *Path of the Paddle.* Willowdale, ON, Canada: Firefly Books, 1999.

Mason, Bill. *Song of the Paddle.* Willowdale, ON, Canada: Firefly Books, 1997.

Ray, Slim. *Canoe Handbook.* Mechanicsburg, PA: Stackpole Books, 1992.

Kayaking: Whitewater

Beazley, Bob. *Kayaking Essentials.* Birmingham, AL: Menasha Ridge Press, 1995.

Dutky, Paul. *Bombproof Roll & Beyond.* Birmingham, AL: Menasha Ridge Press, 1993.

Ford, Kent. *Kayaking (Outdoor Pursuits Series).* Champaign, IL: Human Kinetics Publishers, 1995.

Foster, Tom and Kel Kelly. *Catch Every Eddy, Surf Every Wave.* Millers Falls, MA: Outdoor Center of New England, 1995.

Jackson, Eric. *Playboating: Moves & Training.* Mechanicsburg, PA: Stackpole Books, 2000.

Jackson, Eric. *Whitewater Paddling: Strokes & Concepts*. Mechanicsburg, PA: Stackpole Books, 1999.

Lessels, Bruce. *AMC Whitewater Handbook*. Boston: Appalachian Mountain Club Books, 1994.

Rowe, Ray. *Adventure Sports: White Water Kayaking*. Mechanicsburg, PA: Stackpole Books, 1989.

Kayaking: Sea and Touring

Diaz, Ralph. *The Complete Folding Kayaker*. Rockport, ME: Ragged Mountain Press, 1994.

Dowd, John. *Sea Kayaking*. Seattle: University of Washington Press, 1997.

Foster, Nigel. *Nigel Foster's Sea Kayaking*. Old Saybrook, CT: The Globe Pequot Press, 1997.

Foster, Nigel. *Nigel Foster's Surf Kayaking*. Old Saybrook, CT: The Globe Pequot Press, 1998.

Hutchinson, Derek C. *Complete Book of Sea Kayaking*. Old Saybrook, CT: The Globe Pequot Press, 1995.

Hutchinson, Derek C. *Expedition Kayaking*. Old Saybrook, CT: The Globe Pequot Press, 1999.

Washburne, Randel. *The Coastal Kayaker's Manual*. Old Saybrook, CT: The Globe Pequot Press, 1998.

Sit-on-Tops

Beazley, Bob. *Open-Cockpit Kayaks*. Birmingham, AL: Menasha Ridge Press, 1996.

Holtey, Tom. *Sit-on-Top Kayaking*. Rochester, NY: Geo Odyssey Publications, 1998.

Holtey, Tom. *Tandem Sit-on-Top Kayaking.* Rochester, NY: Geo Odyssey Publications, 1998.

Rafting

Addison, Graeme. *Whitewater Rafting: Essential Guide to Equipment, and Techniques.* Mechanicsburg, PA: Stackpole Books, 2001.

Armstead, Lloyd D. *Whitewater Rafting in North America, 2d edition.* Old Saybrook, CT: The Globe Pequot Press, 1997.

Bennett, Jeff. *Complete Whitewater Rafter.* Rockport, ME: Ragged Mountain Press, 1996.

Kuhne, Cecil. *Inflatable Kayaking: The Complete Guide.* Mechanicsburg, PA: Stackpole Books, 1999.

General Interest Paddling

Bechdel, Les and Slim Ray. *River Rescue: A Manual for Whitewater Safety, 3d edition.* Boston: Appalachian Mountain Club Books, 1997.

Davidson, James and John Rugge. *Complete Wilderness Paddler.* New York: Vintage Books, 1983.

Gullion, Laurie. *The ACA's Kayak and Canoe Games.* Springfield, VA: American Canoe Association, 1996.

Gullion, Laurie, ed. *Canoeing and Kayaking for Persons with Physical Disabilities: Instruction Manual.* Springfield, VA: American Canoe Association, 1990.

About the Authors

Bruce Lessels and *Karen Blom* run Zoar Outdoor, an outdoor center in western Massachusetts specializing in paddlesport instruction and equipment. Bruce was third at the 1987 World Whitewater Championships and coach of the 1988 U.S. Junior World Championship Team. Karen runs several paddling programs for kids in western Massachusetts and was a trainer for the 1989 U.S. Whitewater Team. They live near the Deerfield River with their two children and their collection of kayaks and canoes.

About the Contributing Writers

Frank Bell Jr. has been the director of Camp Mondamin for Boys since 1973—an outdoor adventure camp started by his father in 1922. Under his guidance the camp has produced many well-known paddlers and introduced countless others to the joys of paddling.

Kent Ford's company, Performance Video, is the industry leader in paddling-instruction videos. He has been a member and coach of the U.S. Whitewater Team.

James McEwan's four children paddle canoes, kayaks, and rafts. He and his son, Deven, are currently members of the U.S. Whitewater Team in tandem canoe.

Becky Molina is a mother, an American Canoe Association Instructor Trainer Educator, and a classroom teacher with a master's degree in child development. She specializes in teaching paddling to children

Mark Moore is a professional outdoor educator for more than twenty years, has taught paddling and led wilderness expeditions from Baja, Mexico, to Alaska and Newfoundland. He is the founding member of the National Outdoor Leadership School's Whitewater program, an

ACA Canoe and Kayak Instructor Trainer Educator, an expedition leader of the Trans Borneo Whitewater Exploratin, and Instructor of St. Albans/National Cathedral School's Voyageur Program in Washington, DC, for twelve years. Currently, he operates an outdoor education program from his home in Vermont.

Cindy Ross is the author of six books, including *Kids in the Wild: A Family Guide to Outdoor Adventure* (The Mountaineers Books). Ragged Mountain/McGraw Hill Books will publish her latest book, *Scraping Heaven: A Family's Journey Across the Continental Divide,* in 2002. She lives in Pennsylvania with her husband, Todd Galdfelter, and her children, Sierra and Bryce.

Alison Sparks is an avid sea kayaker who was determined not to stop paddling when her two children were born.

Ken Stone is the father of three accomplished whitewater slalom paddlers and has been the coach of many more. He presently runs the paddling program at Salisbury School in Connecticut.

About the
Appalachian Mountain Club

Since 1876, the Appalachian Mountain Club has helped
people experience the majesty and solitude of the
Northeast outdoors. We offer outdoor skills workshops,
guided trips, and lodging options for all levels of outdoor
adventuring. Our programs include trail maintenance, air
and water quality research, and conservation advocacy work to preserve
the special outdoor places we love and enjoy for future generations.

Join the Club!

Take a hike, ride a bike, paddle a canoe. We believe that people who enjoy
climbing mountains, splashing in streams, and walking on trails have
more fun and take better care of the outdoors. Join the fun today. Call
617-523-0636 or visit www.outdoors.org for membership information.
AMC members receive discounts on workshops, lodging, and books.

Outdoor Adventures

From beginner backpacking to advanced backcountry skiing to guided
hiking and paddling trips, we teach outdoor skills workshops to suit your
interest and experience. Our outdoor education centers guarantee year-
round adventures. View our entire listing of workshops online at
www.outdoors.org.

Huts, Lodges, and Visitor Centers

With accommodations throughout the Northeast, you don't have to travel to the ends of the earth to experience unique wilderness lodging. Accessible by car or on foot, our lodges and huts are perfect for families, couples, groups, and individuals. For reservations call 800-262-4455.

Books and Maps

We can lead you to the best hiking, biking, skiing, and paddling destinations from Maine to North Carolina. With more than fifty books and maps published, we're your definitive resource for discovering wonderful outdoor places. To receive a free catalog call 800-262-4455 or visit our online store at www.outdoors.org.

Contact Us

Appalachian Mountain Club
5 Joy Street
Boston, MA 02108-1490
617-523-0636
www.outdoors.org

Leave No Trace

The Appalachian Mountain Club is a national educational partner of Leave No Trace, a nonprofit organization dedicated to promoting and inspiring responsible outdoor recreation through education, research, and partnerships. The Leave No Trace Program seeks to develop wildland ethics—ways in which people think and act in the outdoors to minimize their impacts on the areas they visit and to protect our natural resources for future enjoyment. Leave No Trace unites four federal land management agencies—the U.S. Forest Service, National Park Service, Bureau of Land Management, and U.S. Fish and Wildlife Service—with manufacturers, outdoor retailers, user groups, educators, organizations like the AMC and the National Outdoor Leadership School (NOLS), and individuals.

The Leave No Trace ethic is guided by these seven principles:

- *Plan ahead and prepare.*
- *Travel/camp on durable surfaces.*
- *Dispose of waste properly.*
- *Be considerate of other visitors.*
- *Minimize campfire impacts.*
- *Respect wildlife.*
- *Leave what you find.*

The AMC has joined NOLS—a recognized leader in wilderness education and a founding partner of Leave No Trace—as the sole national providers of the Leave No Trace Master Educator course through 2004. The AMC offers this five-day course, designed especially for outdoor professionals and land managers, as well as the shorter two-day Leave No Trace Trainer course at locations throughout the Northeast. For information about these Leave No Trace courses visit www.outdoors.org. To register for a course, call 603-466-2727.

Contact *Leave No Trace* at:

P.O. Box 997
Boulder, CO 80306
800-332-4100
www.LNT.org